Henry Collins

Life of Dame Gertrude More, Order of St. Benedict

Henry Collins

Life of Dame Gertrude More, Order of St. Benedict

ISBN/EAN: 9783741194115

Manufactured in Europe, USA, Canada, Australia, Japa

Cover: Foto ©Lupo / pixelio.de

Manufactured and distributed by brebook publishing software (www.brebook.com)

Henry Collins

Life of Dame Gertrude More, Order of St. Benedict

LIFE
OF
DAME GERTRUDE MORE.

[Copyright reserved.]

LIFE

OF

DAME GERTRUDE MORE,

ORDER OF S. BENEDICT.

[*FROM ANCIENT MSS.*]

BY THE REV. FATHER COLLINS,
AUTHOR OF
"THE CISTERCIAN FATHERS," "DAME GERTRUDE
MORE'S DEVOTIONS," ETC., ETC.

LONDON:
THOMAS RICHARDSON AND SONS,
26, PATERNOSTER ROW;
AND DERBY.

IMPRIMATUR.

Nihil obstat.
EDUARDUS B. DOUGLASS, Cen. Dep.

Imprimatur.
✠ EDUARDUS EPISCOPUS
   Nottinghamiensis.

CONTENTS.

Introduction ... PAGE 1

CHAPTER I.
The family and early years of Gertrude More; her entrance into a Convent and Profession ... 13

CHAPTER II.
Her unhappy state of mind, and her attempts at prayer ... 28

CHAPTER III.
She goes to Father Baker for counsel. — His method with her ... 36

CHAPTER IV.
The propension of the soul towards God.—Change in Dame Gertrude More ... 56

CHAPTER V.
Further explanation of the aptitude for an interior life.—The office of an external guide ... 67

CONTENTS.

CHAPTER VI.

Different kinds of prayer for beginners: vocal prayer; meditation, interior acts 76

CHAPTER VII.

Prayer of sensible affections.—Contemplation ... 93
Scheme of Father Baker's teaching on Divine calls 106

CHAPTER VIII.

The call of God to the use of things indifferent.—The soul to proceed gradually 108

CHAPTER IX.

Too much haste hurtful.—Examen of conscience, in what manner made by contemplative souls 117

CHAPTER X.

The aridity in prayer felt by Gertrude.—Her temptation to reiterate former confessions ... 136

CHAPTER XI.

Her sickness and last end ... 145

INTRODUCTION.

The soul of man is in itself simple, having no divisible parts. Yet, man having been created with a nature at once animal, rational, and spiritual, its activities are not simple. They are, on the contrary, capable of a threefold division.* Man's soul lives an animal life, as being connected with an organic body. It is not the body of man which in itself feels pleasure or pain. It is the soul of man

---

* St. Paul's threefold division of man is into σαρκικὸς, ψυχικὸς, πνευματικὸς; or again, body, soul and spirit. Deus rationalem condidit animam, quæ infra sese, sensativa, in se rationalis, supra se spiritalis est. (Rusbrochius de Vera Contemplatione, ch. 68.)

The highest division is also sometimes called the fund of the soul, sometimes the essence of the soul; the memory, understanding and will, being contained in this simple essence, and proceeding forth from it as from their source.

which feels these things through the body. The pleasures of the animal life lie principally in the alternation of activity and quietude of the blood. The blood is roused to a pleasurable excitement by food, by violent exercise, by heat, and other causes. Eating and drinking, ease or exercise, coolness after heat, and warmth after cold, with the pleasures attached to the use of the senses, the animal affections and passions, form this lowest life in which the soul exercises her activities.

The senses of the body, the imagination and memory, are the intelligence of the animal life; and this imagination and memory are the links which connect the animal life in man with the rational life, which comes next in the rising scale of his activities. In the memory are conserved those images or species, which have reached the imagination, through the senses. Fancy, which at will regroups these images, and calls them back before the mind's eye, abstracting this or that as it pleases, is peculiar to the rational nature. The comparing one with another, and separating that, in which they agree as common, as also the discerning in what point one differs from another:—these are exercises of the rational faculties. Abstract ideas grow out of this process, going a further step still from the mere animal powers. Reasoning, or the forming fresh conclusions from these abstract ideas, is the grand mark which distinguishes man, as a rational creature, from the rest of the animal creation.

The rational powers find their first exercise in the accrescence of new ideas. Novelties and curiosities are their exciting food. Most men get but little above this stage. Their highest exercise is to measure and comprehend things that are finite. The attributes of God, as comprehended by these faculties, are certain created images or ideas, abstracted from the infinite.* Go beyond this, and you en-

* See Ruisbroek's "Regnum Amantium Deum," cap. xxxiv.

ter upon a more sublime sphere, the region of the spirit. It is to the spirit that are made known the things of God, revealed to it by God's own Spirit. Its mystic intelligence apprehends that which the reasoning powers cannot reach, namely, the infinite in itself, the unchangeable, the eternal. It takes cognisance of that which is above reason, above all mode, or form, or measure. What is rational can be measured by the reason of man, can be comprehended. God may be apprehended, but not comprehended, by the spirit of man. The knowledge which the spirit has of God is not clear, but obscure, mysterious. This happens partly through the incomprehensibility of God's nature, partly through the cloud on the intelligence of man's spirit, occasioned by the fall, and partly because this intelligence itself is so subtle, compared with the grosser and more palpable knowledge which the rational powers have of the objects of their ken. Whatever then can be known fully and clearly, is not in the region of the spirit, but lower down.

One and the same soul exercises these three activities in the complex nature of man. The animal life has its own energies, its outgoings and its inlets. Sensible objects operate on it, and influence it. The rational portion of man exercises its life in the region of thoughts and ideas, seeking for truth which is its object. The super-rational intelligence has its contact with the infinite, the unmeasured. It is acted on immediately by the Divine Spirit. When any one of these activities immensely predominates, it impresses its peculiar character in a marked manner upon the whole man; but is to be seen especially in the face, the index of the mind. Thus one who is a slave to the pleasures of the body gets an animal, sensual, or even brutish look: one whose whole energies are given to mental pursuits, gets an intellectual-looking face. One who lives in divine things, gets on his face a halo of sanctity. But in the generality of men, in whom there is a moderate activity of all the three energies, nothing marked is to be observed.

In Adam, before the fall, the lower activities did not interfere with the freedom of the spirit. All three then worked in strictest harmony together, the lower being subject to the higher, the bodily appetites to reason, and the rational faculties concording with the spirit. Now each of these lower activities wishes to domineer, sometimes one, sometimes the other, to the sad detriment of the activity of the spirit. The first endeavour of one who is bent on pursuing a spiritual course must be to bring into narrow limits the lower activities, to bridle them and keep them under strict discipline. This, however, must not be done in an arbitrary manner, squaring all to a written rule, but each one must do it according to the measure of his own call. The cravings of the animal nature, for ease, comfort, and pleasure, and the activity of its passions, must be controlled within bounds. Vices must be absolutely cut off. The pleasures of the senses may be permitted, so far as they subserve to keep the body in tolerable health, and render it capable of ministering to the higher activities of the mind and spirit. They are not to be pursued as an end, or for themselves alone. In this matter some require more, some less, and each one must observe his own call. The rational powers require also to be brought under discipline. The craving to hear news, to read light literature, in which fresh scenes may be brought before the mind, the curiosity to know this or that, and come to the bottom of any matter;—all these things must be schooled to order. They may be permitted, so far as useful to the spirit, or as a necessary recreation of the mind, but full liberty is not to be allowed them. Some persons have a habit of day-dreaming, as it is called, which is extremely injurious to spiritual freedom. The mental powers spend themselves and weary themselves, by recalling and going over again scenes that have occurred in past life, or in picturing scenes which might possibly take place in the future. This is done with no object, but the useless, fruitless, gratification of the mental faculties. Others argue and reason out a question in their minds, considering its *pros* and *cons*, with no ulterior object to be gained.

Sometimes this employment may be of use, but many times not. Others are continually planning in the mind about some scheme or work they are bent on getting accomplished; they go over in mind what they have said and done for its accomplishment. All such things as these, and there are many like, waste the energies of the soul in the useless activity of the rational powers.

The mental faculties, therefore, have to be schooled by being taught to drop out of their grasp all unprofitable thoughts, that the will may get such a mastery over the mind, as to admit or exclude thoughts at pleasure, to call them up or bid them go down at its beck.

In the time of spiritual prayer, the mind must be kept entirely free from all definite thoughts. When suggestions offer themselves to the mind, and come in contact with it in order to enter, they are to be thrown back, or brushed away, that the mind may be still and calm as a sheet of unruffled water. The spirit then can commune with God, and God with it, a light being in its intelligence, and a yearning movement of love in its will, but nothing more sensible; a prayer having no noise of words without, or the tumult of discourse within.

The spirit, however, does not ordinarily in the first place get its knowledge of God directly from Him. This knowledge is grounded on the perceptions of the mental powers, and that of the mental powers on what is received by the senses. The way in which the soul ascends this scale may be shown by an example. I see a flower. It is a beautiful rose. As I look with wonder at the delicate texture of its petals, and smell the exquisite fragrance that breathes forth from it, the thought comes unbidden into my mind: How different are the products of nature from the things made by the hand of man! How imperfect are the latter by comparison! My mind then rises with wonder to the thought of an all-wise, all-powerful Creator. The seeing the flower, is the act of the animal nature. The scrutinising of its beauty, and comparing it with things of artificial manufacture, is the act of the rational powers. The thought of the infinitely wise and powerful, is the inference of the intelligence of the spirit. Again, I visit this rose day after day, admiring its beauty. One day, as I am looking at it, a petal falls to the ground. Poor rose, I say, poor rose, so your day is over. Why do I say "poor rose"? Why do I sigh within me at the thought of its short-lived career? It is the thought of eternity that suggests itself to me, the day that shall never end. That which endures ever, the unchangeable. I need not pity the flower, which has not any perception or feeling of its nothingness; but from seeing in it the finite, I pass on by a sort of induction to the infinite. I yearn for this stability, not so much for it as for myself. This yearning is in me by nature; by revelation I know how to find its satisfaction in God. This yearning is the propension of one created to find his happiness in God, clouded by the fall, but not destroyed.*

Spiritual prayer being above the compass of the mind, seems to it vague and indefinite. This happens partly because in this state of prayer the affections of the soul towards God are so multitudinous and so rapidly changing, the whole soul going forth towards Him, and its affections in quick succession following one another, and interlacing themselves one with the other. The many smiles of the sea are a figure of this prayer, always still, but always in movement. No painter could portray the appearance of the ocean at any

* God created the soul pure, and free from every spot of sin, with a certain instinctive tendency to find its bliss in Him.—*S. Cath. of Genoa.*

given moment, for before he has time to fix it in his mind, a change has passed on it. It has lost the particular phase of the moment. The nearest apprehension the mind can form of the state of the soul in this kind of prayer, is to be found in the consideration of those aspirations, which, when in the act of descending from her height, the soul gives birth to. These aspirations are not of the prayer itself, but they are closely connected with it, resulting from it, as its legitimate fruit. Thus spontaneously rising out of a full heart overflowing with love, there is to be seen in them some sort of approximation to the pure prayer of the spirit. But the rational powers can give no adequate expression to the prayer itself. They cannot even form a clear conception of it, so high is it above their reach. When they attempt to search into its nature, they return back bewildered by the scrutiny. This kind of prayer is the one, to which Dame Gertrude More was led by Father Baker's teaching.

THE LIFE
OF
DAME GERTRUDE MORE.

CHAPTER I.

THE FAMILY AND EARLY YEARS OF GERTRUDE MORE; HER ENTRANCE INTO A CONVENT AND PROFESSION.

THE parents of Gertrude More were devout Catholics, and descended of two worshipful families, professors and confessors of the faith in England. Her father was Mr. Cresacre More, the lineal heir of the renowned martyr Sir Thomas More, and possessor of so much of his lands as were restored to his family by the most virtuous Queen Mary of England, the residue of his possessions being alienated by her predecessors, to strangers. He was the son of Thomas, son and heir of John, the son and heir of Sir Thomas More; so Sir

Thomas More was his great grandfather. The name of Cresacre was given him on his Christening, in memory of a family of the surname of Cresacre, seated in Yorkshire, not far from Doncaster. The heir, who was a female of that family, being married to John, the eldest son of Sir Thomas More, from this couple descended Mr. Cresacre More, with his brothers and sisters. The possessions of that family were the chief part of his revenues, the greater part of Sir Thomas More's possessions remaining alienated from the race by the confiscation upon his attainder.

Her mother was sister to Sir John Gage, of Firle, in Sussex, Knight and Baronet, lineal heir and inheritor in possessions to Sir John Gage, for many years comptroller of King Henry VIII's. household, and after by good Queen Mary made Lord Chamberlain of her household. This Sir John was by her much employed against Wyat, the heretical rebel, she reposing much confidence in him for his known sincerity in faith, which in those days faltered in many, even of the greatest persons in England. Her parents were both devout Christians, and of exemplary lives. Her mother lived not many years after marriage, but died leaving a son and two daughters, whereof the one was the good soul of whom the following pages treat, and the other was her sister, Dame Bridget More, who was likewise a Nun, professed at the same house at Cambray.

Dame Gertrude was not above four or five years old when her mother died, and she had her education till she came to Religion almost wholly with, and under, her father. She was born at Lowe Luton, a house of her father's in Essex, upon the 25th of March, being the feast of the Annunciation of the Blessed Virgin, in the year of our Lord 1606, and Christened by the name of Helen, in regard perhaps of St. Helen, mother of Constantine the Great, whom the county of Essex doth challenge to have been born in the town of Malden there. But she, coming to Religion, chose the name of Gertrude, as the common use is to change names upon entering into Religion, out of the honour she bore to that name, that had yielded divers Saints in our Order, especially to the great S. Gertrude. It is no great marvel that an extraordinary good soul should proceed from so devout a family; for, besides that her mother was a very devout woman, her father, and his two brothers, and all his sisters, being many, were very devout spirits. Mr. Cresacre More was the youngest son; Mr. Thomas More, one of the brothers, became a priest, and died at Rome, being agent and procurator there, at his own expense, for the secular clergy of England. Another brother was professed of the Order of S. Francis of Paula, called Minims, at Amiens, and there died. Mr. Cresacre himself lived in the English seminaries for the space of ten years, and there studied philosophy and divinity with the intention of becoming a Churchman. But having then alive an elder brother, that was reserved to be inheritor of the father, and yet happened to die before the father, Mr. Cresacre was by the father and other of his friends sent for to come to England, and persuaded to marry, to preserve the property in the name and in the family of Catholics, he being as yet capable, and the other brothers incapable. As for the sisters, who were many in number, most of them married. But all of them, in their several conditions, were women of much prayer and piety. Mr. Cresacre was very unwilling to enter on the state of marriage, but yet suffered himself to be overruled by the counsel of others. But his wife dying in four or five years, he would not marry again, though he was young and of a very healthy constitution of body. He lived a single life for more than six-and-twenty years. His only son, upon the like ground as his father, sought to escape marriage as much as he could, and fled away for that end, choosing rather to become a Religious; but at length he yielded to the contrary by persuasion of his friends. The other daughter, Dame Bridget More, who was three or four years younger than Dame Gertrude, and remained in the world after her, though she was much sought after for marriage, and her father both very able and willing to give a great portion with her, yet would not yield to marry, but chose the Religious state, and at the age of eighteen years came to her sister at Cambray, and there was professed a Nun, with satisfaction to her own soul and edification to others.

It is not well to pass over unmentioned the singular piety and religion of the father and mother of Mr. Cresacre More, and of his brothers and sisters. His mother being a Scroope, of the honourable family of the

Lords Scroope. They were both of them wonderfully devout Christians, lived long, and suffered a persecution most grievous and long all Queen Elizabeth's days. They brought up their children, who were many, very piously, and at their own charge maintained their sons at the English college at Rheims. Their daughters, though of religious spirits, entered not into houses of Religion, partly because there were not such houses in England extant in those days, and partly because the religious state for women was not then well known or understood in England, and the use of older days in that point was now forgotten.

Dame Gertrude remained in England, for the most part residing with her father, till she came to the age of eighteen years. During this period I have little to say concerning her; partly because I did not then know her, and partly because by what I have heard of her, there was not much then supernatural in her, nor anything very notable in her as regards religion. But she was of a very good nature, gentle, affable, kind, tractable, merry, and pleasant; very forward in natural wit and judgment for her years. Her father so delighted in her company and conversation, that his life, which was otherwise solitary, was the more tolerable and pleasing to him. He loved her so well, he had determined to have bestowed a liberal portion for her marriage. The reverend father who was then her confessor, being a grave Benedictine father, Father Bennet Jones, observing in her the said good dispositions, proposed to her to enter a monastic state, of which she had little before heard. But neither of them would as yet determine what were best for her to do in the matter, because she seemed not sufficiently to understand the nature of a religious state, at least not the aptness of it for herself.

But, in fine, after consultations between her and her natural and spiritual fathers, two or three years after such proposing and consultation, the resolution and conclusion was that she should make trial of the Religious life, to proceed in it or not as upon experience she should see cause. The said father had then under his charge, and of his acquaintance in England, some others of the same sex, who desired to be Nuns of the Benedictine Order, and of his particular congregation.

Whereupon the father, consulting upon it

with her father, Mr. More and herself, (he not having at that time any house of women subject to his congregation,) it was concluded that Mr. More should give a competent portion with his daughter, for the foundation of a Convent of women. This, together with the lesser portions which those others had who meant to join, was esteemed to be sufficient for the formation of the new cloister.

Thereupon, accordingly, not long after, viz., in the summer of 1623, Gertrude More, and eight other English gentlewomen, came over for this purpose, under the conduct of Father Bennet Jones, to Douay. They lived together there, merely as seculars, in a fair house belonging to the abbey of St. Voust, in Arras. For this they had the permission of the Right Rev. Philip Caverell, then Lord Abbot, until they should have a convenient house of their own provided for them. Whilst there Gertrude More was visited with a grievous sickness, which brought her into some peril of death, but it pleased God to restore her to health.

There being some hopes of obtaining a house at Cambray, they all went there shortly after, and were there entertained, as seignioresses, in the house of the Hospital of St. James, till they might be provided with a house of their own. The situation of the proposed house was thought very convenient for them, and the Archbishop Vandeburgh was so gracious to them, that he not only favoured their admittance into the house, but also willingly granted to them exemption from himself and his successors, in order to further their immediate subjection to the congregation.

Gertrude was now in the midst of the seventeenth year of her age. She still remained in her former purpose of making trial of the Religious life, without further determining as yet as to whether she should ultimately embrace it, but referring all to experience, and to what she might ascertain to be for her God's will. The father, that came with them out of England, after some time spent at Cambray, returned to England, and the Rev. Father who was then president of the congregation, took upon him the immediate care of them.

About All Hallowtide, following their arrival at Cambray, three Religious dames, whom our fathers had procured from the English

Benedictine Nunnery at Brussels, to come and help in the erecting of the new Nunnery at Cambray. These three were Dame Frances Gascoine, Dame Potentiana Decons, and Dame Virginia Yasley.

Meantime the Benedictine fathers had obtained from the Abbot of S. Andrew's, a Monastery of their Order at Cambray, for the use of our intended Nuns, a certain house at Cambray, which belonged to the Abbey of Semey, an abbey united to that of S. Andrew's.

The Most Rev. Anthony de Montmorenci, being Abbot then, allowed them to have it for their use. It is reported that the Abbey of Semey was itself founded by three Englishmen. The said house, or refuge, having been first adapted for the use of our Nuns, they all entered in and began their habitation there, upon Sunday, the 14th of December, in the year 1623. The Archbishop honoured their entry with his presence, and upon that day said mass there in the chapel, being the first mass that ever was said there. The Sunday following, being the feast of the Circumcision of our Lord, the aforesaid nine were publicly and solemnly vested with the holy habit by

the Lord Archbishop, the Very Rev. Father
Rudismede Barlowe, then President of our
Congregation, being also present. Of these
matters, Dame Gertrude says as follows in a
memorandum.

"I entered the Monastery of our Blessed
Lady, (for to that Monastery of theirs at
Cambray had been given the name of our
Blessed Lady of Comfort,) the 24th of December, being Sunday, and I took the habit
the 31st of the same month and year. I was
professed in 1625, on the feast of the Holy
Name of Jesus, being that year on a Wednesday, and it being the year of jubilee. I
was then eighteen years old, and as much as
from the 24th of March."

The names of the nine that took the habit
are the following: Dame Gertrude, who had
the first place. Margaret Vavasour, daughter
of Mr. William Vavasour, of Hazelwood, in
Yorkshire, who now chose the name of Lucy.
Anne, now called Benedicta Morgan, sister to
Mr. Thomas Morgan, of Weston, in the county
of Warwick. Catherine Gascoigne, daughter
of Mr. John Gascoigne, of Barnelowe, in Yorkshire. Grace, now called Agnes More and
Anne More, cousins of Gertrude, and descended

also from Sir Thomas More. Frances, now called Mary Watson, daughter of Mr. Richard Watson, of —— Park, in Bedfordshire. Sister Mary Hoskins, and Sister Jane Martin. These two were lay sisters, the rest were for the Choir.

The said Sister Jane Martin had taken the name Martha, and being professed at the year's end with the rest, she lived five or six years after her profession, and then happily died, and is buried in the nunnery of Dremea, of the order of St. Augustine, or Canons Regular, at Cambray.

Dame Gertrude More, and another nun of the house, called Ebba Browne, were buried there too, because as yet they had no place of burial in or about their own dwelling house. These three buried at Dremea have over their bodies three stones of marble, with engravings signifying the persons there buried.

Dame Frances Gascoine, one of the three that came from Brussels, was their first Abbess. Mr. More loved his daughter Gertrude as affectionately as any father could love his child, and she loved him as affectionately as any child could love her father, so that their separation must needs have been painful to them both. She was naturally exceedingly affectionate to kindred and friends, and therefore it was but consonant to her spirit and nature, that being once converted to God, she should prove very affectionate and amorous towards Him.

That loving propension towards Him, which will appear in the sequel of her life, she had, partly by grace, and partly by the nature of her temperament, by whose qualities the intellectual soul seems to be in some measure affected. Now that she is brought into the Monastery, enclosed, vested, and placed under a President, Confessor and Abbess, it will be necessary next to show how matters stood with her in such state of Religion, and what amount of call she had to Religion.

It is plain she had no great call to the world, for she neither desired marriage nor the riches and honours of the world. Still, while she lived in the world, it does not seem there was any very great devotion in her to God and divine matters. For her faith, a good believer she always was. She was also of a gentle and pleasing nature and harmless carriage, of a quick, sharp wit, and good judgment for her years. She lived till she entered her seventeenth year in tolerable innocence and simplicity; being for the most part brought up in her father's house, where there was great piety exercised, and all good order kept, where no evil examples or company could draw her astray.

In the book of her confessions, she thus commends the care her father took of her. "Certainly my sins," she says, "deserved to be punished in an extraordinary manner, because I committed them more wilfully than people ordinarily do. The carefulness of Thy servant my father, that I should be kept out of all occasions of sin was such that I might, considering also the nature Thou gavest me, have lived very innocently."

And a little after, she says: "I beseech Thee remember Thy true servant my father, who, through his care, prevented my further evil."

When she first came to the trial of the Religious state, she appears to have been in ignorance of its real nature, knowing nothing but by imagination and hearsay, by means of which she could form no judgment, nor did she determine on anything till she came to make her profession. It would seem, then, that at first she had no absolute call to Religion that she could perceive. But when she had entered into a place of more retiredness and devotion, she became much better disposed for Religion.

Accordingly, when the time of her profession came, she made, probably, a conscientious choice of the Religious state; this, perhaps, led more by natural judgment and election, than out of any divine interior call that she could discern. By what follows, it may be concluded that she had a real call, but was not yet in the disposition to discern it.

CHAPTER II.

HER UNHAPPY STATE OF MIND, AND HER ATTEMPTS AT PRAYER.

Being professed, God gave to Dame Gertrude the grace to have a great desire to serve Him in the best manner. For this she had many advantages, external and internal. She was a good Choir Nun, having a voice well adapted for singing or reciting.

She took pleasure in singing, and had a pretty strong voice. A good wit and judgment she had; indeed, extraordinary for her sex and years. She was also now in a place and state wherein she had few impediments, and all the helps to devotion usually to be found in contemplative Orders.

Her call and aptitude certainly were for an internal life. Had she not embraced it, her soul would never have been happy in Religion, nor would others have been satisfied with her. The difficulty, however, with her, was how to get into her interior, so as to learn to lead an internal life, the name of which she had scarcely heard of; and much less she knew as yet what it meant. She had two wants; the first was the want of a teacher. She must be taught, either by God or by man, how to enter within her interior, for by herself she could not learn it, no more can any soul.

The second want was of a suitable habitude of mind. She was of a most extroverted disposition, of a very curious, stirring, and working imagination; prone to conversations, to solicitudes, recreations, and to all such kind of extroversions as had no sin in them; and no friend was she to solitude and silence.

She had now also grown to be over scrupulous in some things, which was a further impediment to an internal life. How to bring one of such a nature and disposition into the course of an internal life, was indeed a huge difficulty, both for speculation and practice.

Natural reason and the light of grace, which she had, made her put little or no perfection in external things. Nevertheless, though she had small account of them, yet she performed them in the best manner she could. But her soul was nothing satisfied with them, nor with all she did in them.

This dissatisfaction had for its root and ground, probably, those primary motions of the Divine Spirit, which inclined her to aspire after a spiritual union with God.

She knew that a truly Religious life chiefly consists in the interior, but not understanding how to find her way to this interior spirit, she lived, as it were of necessity, a life wholly extroverted, though in Religion, and enclosed; and though, also, she performed all the external observances of the rule, and the orders of the superiors. Thus she lived a discontented life in her interior, and felt daily an increase of guilt in her conscience, on account of her increase in daily imperfections. She grew, indeed, more imperfect every day, becoming more remote from God and the sight of her interior. The disposition of her heart, which in the world was simple and good, now turned to be full of craftiness and other defectuosities. For not learning what was good in Religion, her intelligence found another channel for its activity. She learned all those arts and stratagems by which relaxed Religious manage to secure their own ends and conveniences in houses where there is no true spirituality, or the practice of abnegation.

She thus lost that simplicity which she had brought with her out of the world. Her nature was much altered for the worse, and being retired in her cell, a thing, indeed, which happened rarely, unless at bed time, then she reflected on herself, and, seeing her own misery, bitterly bemoaned her case. She saw in herself a thing others might have observed also, namely, a sad decay in natural and moral virtues. God gave her, at this time, a great good-will to do better, to amend all, and to tend to perfection.

But she knew not how to do it, on account of the wants and impediments before specified, yet she did the best she could, as far as her knowledge went, using all industry, but it availed little or nothing. Where she could open her mind, and secretly treat with such as she loved to be inward with, she drew no good to herself. On the contrary, by these familiarities, she did herself a great deal of harm, taking occasion through them, of venting out her griefs, discontentments, murmurings and passions. By such like means of extroversion, she lost the benefit of all the good motions and inspirations she had, when she was private to herself, or at her devotions.

God, however, gave her a very strong good will for the amending of all; and through this good will she sought after every means of bettering her state, which natural reason could suggest for her help. She read over, for this purpose, all the books that were in the house, or that she could get from abroad, printed and manuscript, and read them seriously. In particular, she read over the whole English Bible privately to herself, from the very beginning to the end, both the Old and New Testament, besides what she read by parcels at other times. When she heard of any spiritual persons, whom she imagined to be likely to be able to put her in a good way, she sought counsel of them, if she could have access to them. She requested to know of them the most necessary points for her, to wit: in what perfection consists, and by what means and exercises she should tend towards it; what practices the Saints and good persons in the Benedictine and other Orders used, in order to attain sanctity and perfection.

She desired, after her manner, and according to the desire and good will God had given her, to aim at the same excellence of life. Such questions, then, she proposed to them, and with a depth of wit and judgment, that some of her Confessors had enough to do to come off with answers that themselves might think satisfactory. Her case she herself thus speaks of in her own writings: "I had suffered so much, and fell into so many inconveniences and miseries, before God did bestow on me the favour of being put into a course that was proper for me, that it would be hardly credible to any one but myself who knew it. This state of things lasted for nearly three years. And though I made a shift in the day time to set a good face on it, yet at night I bewailed my miseries, with more than ordinary tears, which God and our Blessed Lady were witness of, but few else on earth were aware of: and yet in those times I hunted up all the books in the house; and whatsoever I found that one had done to please God, I took notes of it, and practised it myself as well as I could. I used also to consult all the spiritual men I could meet with, but all this did me no good, and methought I was as great a stranger to Almighty God, as I was when in England. Being thus perplexed with a thousand imaginations, my mistress advised me to go to Father Augustin Baker, telling me that four or five in the house had been benefited by so doing, and at least there was no harm in my trying my fortune with him too."

In the days of her Noviceship she used vocal prayers, and other external devotions, in Choir and out of Choir, as much as others did. These exercises gave her no internal light or satisfaction to her soul. She was counselled to use meditation or discursive prayer, but she found herself utterly unable for it; nor could she use any kind of internal consideration that would move, or better her affection to God, or otherwise help her to pray.

This same incapability on this point remained in her, even to her death. She never could discourse on, or consider internally, spiritual matters, so as thereby to raise up devout affections towards God. She much desired to be able, and often attempted it, but always failed.

It was not that she was defective in her imagination, or other mental faculties, for she could well ponder on and consider to and fro any matter that had no relation to prayer. She reasoned indeed with wonderful power and judgment, considering her years and sex, and that she had not been brought up in the subtleties of human learning. But to move the will by the help of considerations, was with her an utter impossibility, and she received no benefit by her attempts at discursive prayer. She had several other seemingly repugnant qualities in her character. For example, none was more timorous in conscience as to some points than she, and as to others, none freer or bolder; none more cheerful and merry, yet none more subject to sadness, or more easily cast into it; none more prone to extroversions than she, yet none with a greater call and aptness for a true interior spirit. Also, after she was come into a more spiritual way in the time of internal lights, which were frequent, she had lights most perspicuous and clear; at other times, which were frequent, she was in great obscurity of soul. Her remedy then was, that she stood in practice to such lights as she had had in more clarity of soul.

CHAPTER III.

SHE GOES TO FATHER BAKER FOR COUNSEL.— HIS METHOD WITH HER.

Now it fell out in the year of her Noviceship, when Gertrude was yet in the miserable case above described, that the Rev. Father Baker arrived at Cambray, being appointed by his superiors to live there for some time. He had left England to shun for a time the heat of a persecution that was much threatened. This persecution was looked for owing to a proclamation lately sent forth for the banishment of priests. Father Baker, though a priest, and in the mission of England, yet did not busy himself in the work of the mission, but, with leave of his superiors, attended to himself, leading a retired and contemplative life, which he then did, and had done for some years before. He arrived at Cambray the middle of July. By this time the company, or Convent of Nuns, was increased by the arrival of three more, who came in one after another in the beginning of this summer. These three were, Dame Margaret Yasley, who took the name of Placida; Dame Anne Temperlee, who took the name of Scholastica; and Sister Flavie Browne; so that, together with the three that came from Brussels, the whole number amounted to fifteen. Father Baker was, on his arrival, lodged and entertained in the hostrie, outside the Nunnery, and there remained. Some of the Nuns, hearing that he was of a retired and spiritual life, sought to speak with him, and desired some spiritual instructions at his hands, which he accordingly gave them, and for the time they were satisfied with them.

They did not, however, all of them follow out the instructions given, for some conceived these instructions to be unsuitable to their particular character. Now Dame Gertrude More, before she came out of England, had heard of Father Baker, and remembered perfectly well the reputation he had. Still, however, though none in the house stood in greater need of spiritual help than she; yet, of all that were in the house, she was the most backward. She was indeed the very last that went to speak with him. Her reason, as she afterwards acknowledged when she had come to know him better, was because, by what she had heard of him, she conceived him to be a man of a singular course of life, and one, to wit, of much retiredness, a thing she found her own nature utterly averse to; and she said, "What should I do with such a man?" She did not only not seek his advice for herself, but also, out of the imagination she had of some extravagance, or of some peril in his courses, she declared herself against his proceedings. Commonly in any faction or disunion in which she took any part, she, by reason of her wit, her tongue, and animosity, became a sort of chief to others. But, as she was very affable and courteous, she did sometimes, by way of entertainment, go to converse with the Reverend Father. This, however, was but to little purpose as regards the matters of the soul. About the end of November, in the year of her noviceship, she fell dangerously ill. She recovered, however, and was perfectly well again some time before her profession day, which was fixed for the 1st of January, 1625 (stilo Romano). Her eight companions were to be professed with her on the same day, it being then a full year after their clothing. All things were therefore prepared for this event. Gertrude, however, it would appear, was as yet unresolved, or rather in a perplexity what to do, because she had in her certain defects which yet she knew not how to amend. In particular, through immortification of the will, she found a great aversion to obey the Nun that was to be her Superior, that is to say, as a Religious person ought to obey.

On account of this defect it went against her conscience to make a profession, yet had she, for all this, a very good desire to amend, and to seek after God in the best manner. On the other side, she saw many reasons, which indeed were but human reasons, which should urge her to make a profession. One reason might be, because the foundation of the house, for its temporalities, depended greatly upon her portion, and how much of it her father would give to the house if she did not profess was much to be doubted, because she herself must somehow be maintained with a livelihood.

Another reason was, that if she did not profess she knew not well what to do with herself; and as for marrying, she had as little mind for it as ever she had; besides that, the rumour of her becoming a Nun would probably have disabled her from obtaining so good a settlement as otherwise she might have done. For it is held to be a dishonour among our nation, though perhaps with no very great reason, when a gentlewoman puts herself into a Religious house, takes the habit, and does not proceed, especially if she be in health of body, as Gertrude More now was. These three points, with some others of that kind, she herself intimates in one of her confessions, by words to this effect, that the world had now forsaken her.

These considerations, revolved to and fro in her mind, made her, even on the eve of her profession day, to be unresolved what to do in the matter. In conclusion, however, she made her profession with the rest, and had, as she had before, the first place, the forenamed archbishop taking the professions and performing the ceremonies, the Rev. Father President being also present. Gertrude thus made profession of the religious state; but did she merely externally embrace this state, or did she embrace it also in her heart? There is good reason to believe that she, being of an excellent judgment, and tender conscience, and having at least the primary movements of a call from God, as above mentioned, did, in her interior as well as in her exterior, make a deliberate and voluntary profession, though perhaps with no great alacrity, but rather with some fear. She herself, however, after she had entered into the spiritual course, into which she was brought through the instructions of Father Baker, which was long after, became then very discontented with the manner in which she had made her profession. She could not be quiet in mind, or satisfied in her conscience, until the Father President had given her leave to renew her vows privately to him. This he yielded to for her satisfaction, she doing it through a doubt or fear, at least, of the validity of her former profession.

Being now professed in the dispositions above stated, it would appear that at first, and for a time, Gertrude used the more force with herself that she might live, both inwardly and outwardly, in accordance with her profession, to the best of her knowledge and ability. But, not long after, she found herself deeply plunged in her former miseries, which seemed increased by her profession, such as it was, so that she found herself to live after no better fashion, but after rather a worse one than before. Her natural virtues wonderfully decayed, and her heart, as she often professes in her writings, seemed to be grown as hard as a stone in all that concerned God or goodness. It is not possible to imagine a more discontented life than what she was now come to lead, never having been sunk in greater, or so great miseries. Then she fell to bethink herself how she might come to live more contented, though indeed there was but one means for compassing such a thing, and this one was, that she should enter on a spiritual course suited to her, and answerable to the call she had from God.

She was ignorant, however, of this only remedy for her wretched state, and being in despair of obtaining a cure, as having done already all that she could for it, it came into her mind, that if she were removed out of her convent into some other house, then matters might go better with her. Then she thought she should have a Superior more after her own mind, and companions to whom she should not be so much affected as those with whom she was. Through her blindness of mind she could not discern the grossness of the temptation. The only remedy for her wants was a true interior spirit of prayer, and she might just as likely fail of this in one place as in another place.

But she being in these moods about the Whitsuntide next after the profession, there came to visit her at Cambray her own most loving and dearly beloved father Mr. More, who was entertained and lodged in the hostrie of the Nunnery. He remained there two or three months, commonly every day once visiting his daughter, and recreating himself with her. And she, though inwardly as much out of order as ever, yet complied with her father, put a good face upon matters, and gave him the best satisfaction she could. Nevertheless, her interior misery was grown now so great, that it came to her mind to break the matter to her father. She thought to ask him to help her to remove to some other house, where she hoped she might live more contentedly, for that, in her present convent, she found such difficulties as she could neither bear with or overcome. Once she was on the point of opening her mouth to make her request, but her heart, or rather God, would not permit her to do it. If she had done it, her father's affection to her was such that he would certainly have done all that lay in his power to accomplish and satisfy her desire. And much could he have done in the case, all circumstances considered; but, by the providence of God, she did not name anything, though she had an urgent inclination to do so. Had she done so perhaps she would not have found in another house that which was so necessary for her soul, namely, one to direct her into the way of spiritual prayer.

The good providence of God is therefore to be praised. And often afterwards did Gertrude marvel how she had withheld herself from opening that grief which consumed her to such a father; one that was so tender of her, and to whom she could so freely have imparted the very secrets of her soul. But she said that surely it was not God's will that she should do it. And it was He only that restrained her in it.

About the middle of August, in the same summer, Mr. More went away from Cambray to Antwerp to remain for some time there. A little before the profession, or not long after, Gertrude went to Father Baker, who remained at Cambray for more than nine years from the time of his first coming thither, and sought to have some spiritual directions, which he gave her by word of mouth. These instructions had no great effect with her at that time. The chief reason of this probably was, that she had not yet reached the idea of the nature of a true spiritual prayer. Perhaps, too, through ignorance, she did not exert herself as well as she might have done in the business of prayer, by industry and patience, not giving it over on account of interior darkness, or desolations, to which she was much subject.

All her spiritual good and reformation was to proceed from prayer. As yet, however, she was in no way touched for the better by the directions she received from Father Baker, but held on her former course towards him and towards others, mocking and jesting with a fund of wit that was natural to her, at those who followed his instructions. Yet, sometimes observing that those who followed the counsels of Father Baker became both better and happier, she would say to them: "It is well for you that you can get good by them, I can get none." Thus it stood with her till the All Hallowtide following her profession. Then she came to him again, being over-persuaded to do so by the mistress of novices, and he gave her some further directions as to the method of praying most fitting for her. And here lay, indeed, the great difficulty: namely, how to lead her to a prayer that should be suitable to her mind and temperament. Vocal prayer was insufficient for her; meditate she could not, at least not to any good effect. For, though she could form in her mind the images of things, and make mental discourse, yet this did not serve to move her will at all towards God, so as to enable her to break forth into acts of love, but her will would remain as hard and unmoved as if she had but discoursed or preached to a stone.

The case of many good souls is similar to hers, and probably often for the very selfsame reason, so that the remedy that profited her would serve them also. The ground-work of all Gertrude's piety lay in this, that she had, in the fund of her soul, a strong propension to love God, and to make herself over entirely to

Him. This propension existed in her partly through natural character.

Grace, however, doubtless added to what nature had given, awakened as it lay dormant and roused it into activity. This propension, seated in the superior will, urged her to seek after God and eternal happiness, to the disesteem and neglect of the transitory goods of this life. The propension of the will here spoken of, though so strong and efficacious, is extremely obscure and subtle in its nature, and on this account is not easily explicable by words. Its impulses, moreover, are of so primary a character, that, unless the soul that experiences them seconds them by her own positive efforts and action, they remain unfruitful, and are productive of no good. The treatment of this propension towards God and goodness in the soul, ought to be varied according to each one's individual temperament.

The propension itself is the gift of God, through nature and grace, and is the first foundation in the soul of all desires for what is good, holy and pure. Without it she would be utterly dead to the things of God, having no hope or thought of them. This propension, giving her a first ground-work of good, enables her also to develop this good by the exercise of her own activity, but this exercise must vary, as has been said, according to each one's character. In one it must be after this fashion, in another after that. With Gertrude the use of discourse or sensible images was not proper for this purpose. She was called to develop this propension towards God by the exercise of the affections. In this exercise she followed sometimes the suggestions of the interior impulse, moving her to this or that affection. Sometimes she used from memory such aspirations as she had been accustomed to make, or she chose out of a book such aspirations as had a relish for her. She selected, for this end, out of St. Augustine's confessions and meditations, and out of other works of affective prayer, a great store of amorous aspirations, which were admirably suited to give expression to the wants and desires of her soul. By following these exercises she came commonly to have a very efficacious prayer, and one of much recollection. She also gained a great deal of self-knowledge, discovering her inordinate affections and other defects by an interior light, and receiving at the same time strength and grace from

God for the amendment of them. This interior light, together with the propension of the will towards God, aided as it was by grace, now fully satisfied her. For now she found that she was entered on a good way, and all she required was to keep in it. Nevertheless, it frequently fell out that none of those selected amorous aspirations would avail her, nor could she produce them with any gust; but she would be in a dulness, coldness, or stupidity of will. At these times she found herself in some perplexity and difficulty. But being advised by Father Baker, one way or other to stick to her prayer, and not to give it up for any difficulty whatsoever that occurred, she found by experience that even in these desolations, and dulness of will, when she did what she could, she made a spiritual progress. For, through the secret workings of the divine Spirit, she still gained much strength of will, as also a light to discern and amend both present and past defects.

In the beginning of this course of hers, when she was much subject to these desolations, Father Baker was one day reading to her out of a book called "*Hidden Paths of Divine Love.*" Whilst reading he came to the following passage : " There are some who are led by great aridity and indevotion, so that they have no sensible perception of the divine correspondence, and know not which side to turn to obtain help to elevate themselves towards God. Those in such case can do no better, than in their poverty of spirit and aridity, to be contented, doing, nevertheless, the best they can. And then let them comfort themselves with the accomplishment of the divine will, accommodating all their exercises to arrive at the true love of God." When Father Baker had read this and some other things out of the same author, Gertrude, struck with it, suddenly said, "On, on! That may be my way. And I pray you," said she to him, "let me have that place translated into English," for he had read it from a Latin book. Father Baker translated it and gave it to her, and she made use of that doctrine, continuing her prayer with great profit, notwithstanding all her desolations. On the subject of the great change which took place in her, and which has been above described, she herself thus speaks in her own writings : " I had of myself no mind to go to Father Baker, yet upon my mistress bidding me, I went. I received some general instructions from him about prayer and other things, and having put them in practice the best I could, within fifteen days after I found myself so quieted in mind and soul that I wondered at it myself. The instructions which brought about this happy change were, that I must give all to God, without any willing reservation of any inordinate affection to any creature. This I found my soul quite ready to do. Then that I must use mental prayer twice a day. This, too, I found myself capable of, and though I experienced little of that which is called sensible devotion, yet I found that, with a little industry, I was able to use prayer with much more profit; and the use of it made any cross thing which happened very tolerable to me. It made me also capable of understanding what was necessary for me in a spiritual life, discovering to me daily those things that were impediments between God and my soul, and making me abhor the doing a thing for any other end than for God, and because He would have me do it. I find that, by and in this exercise of prayer, God contrives means to humble me, such as all the creatures in the world would never have discovered. He also sends me such internal crosses, and withal shows me so plainly what I should do in them if I would advance by means of them, that it would but tend to obscure my soul to ask questions about them, and, will or nil, I must bear them; and this I see, that God so tempers everything He lays upon me, that it is suitable to me, being just what I am able to bear and no more. I see that any victory I gain is so wholly to be attributed to God, that I should think it an extreme presumption to expose myself to hazard, by the voluntary assumption of any cross or suffering but what obedience or necessity provide for me. These I find to be enough."

In another place she thus compares the system of guidance followed by Father Baker, with that of others. "Some spiritual directors, exacting more than the grace and ability of a simple beginner can achieve, make obedience and other virtues seem an intolerable burthen, and their disciples by such means faint away in the very beginning of their course, when, if only these disciples were brought to do all things with discretion, they would in no long time make rapid progress.

For want of this discretion it falls out, that many times the burthen of religion seems heavy even to good and well-meaning persons. The spiritual guidance, however, of Father Baker was full of this discretion, and in this point differed much, to my seeming, from that of others whom I had before consulted. If he had exacted over much of me, I know that I should never have had heart to persevere. But he daily for a long time encouraged me not to be daunted with my sins and imperfections, assuring me it would all turn to my good, if by prayer I would endeavour to tend to God. He also required me to use the best means I could to reform myself in all inordinate affection to created things. This, however, was to be done more by quietness than by extraordinary force, and he exhorted me to bear with myself and my defects; I could never have held out had he not dealt thus discreetly with me: by the way which he laid down for me those imperfections which I desired to, but could not at first reform, decayed little by little, and fell off when God Almighty, as I may say, saw His own fitting time for it. Now this method of dealing with the soul was quite contrary to the course extolled by some whom I had before met with, who for the most part gave no other advice than to overcome all things by force and violence.* But God showed me plainly, in reading Father Baker's books, that the way for me was to overcome myself, as I could, and not as I would; I mean to say that I must expect God's good pleasure, and that

* St. Teresa makes the same complaint of one of her directors. "He started," she says, "with a holy resolve to direct me, as if I were robust and far advanced......to the end that I might in no way displease the Divine Majesty. When I became aware that he was so resolved upon correcting the smallest faults, from which I wanted strength to set myself free with so much perfection, I conceived great anguish: and observing that he looked on the state of my soul as a state which ought to be thoroughly and at once changed, it seemed to me that I must put in practice a degree of skill and energy beyond that to which I had been accustomed. At length I came to know that the means which he prescribed to me were not those needed for my cure, but that they would, perhaps, have suited some more perfect soul. And certainly, if I had not happened to treat with others besides him, I believe I should never have made any progress in spirit, because the affliction caused by my perceiving that I did not, and, as it seemed to me, could not do what he ordered, was sufficient to make me lose hope and give up everything."—*Scaramelli's Directorium Asceticum*, vol. iii. ch. 7.

then, if I did my best, I should by His grace surmount that which, with all my industry, I was not able of myself to overcome. The practice of this method showed me my own frailty, and how little we are able to do of ourselves, yea, indeed, nothing that is good. For, after having been able to overcome myself in a thing many a time, I have thought myself thereby safe, and able to do it again, then I have failed more deeply than ever before. This causes me never to dare to presume on my own strength in anything how little soever, for if I do, I am sure to fail."

And here end her words.

CHAPTER IV.

THE PROPENSION OF THE SOUL TOWARDS GOD.— CHANGE IN DAME GERTRUDE MORE.

God has placed in the heart of every man a desire of Himself. There are different ways of satisfying this propension of the creature towards the Creator. Some seek after God by activity in external good actions, others by prayer and meditation, with the use of sensible images in the mind. By means of meditative discourse they find their will to be moved towards Him. Gertrude More was not called to this way of approaching God. She had in her a certain loathing of all discourse and exercise of the imagination in this sacred work. Her thirst after God was to find Him imageless in her own interior, not to be drawn to Him by external good deeds, nor by means of meditative discourses.

Many others doubtless have the like call and propension to seek God in their interior, but unfortunately their spiritual intelligence is not sufficiently clear to enable them to discern aright the secret ways, by which the Divine Spirit would guide them. In consequence of this defect they not unfrequently err, by mistaking the leadings of their own imagination for the conduct of the Divine Spirit. It requires a very clear eye to distinguish nicely, at all times, between the motions of nature and the drawings of the Spirit. Where this spiritual intelligence does not exist, all external guides in the world will not be able to supply its defect. Gertrude, however, was happily endued with a great gift of this spiritual discernment. By following Father Baker's instructions, she became disposed for receiving the divine lights; but had she not had the clear spiritual faculties for observing them, this would have profited her little. Father Baker did not pretend to be her chief master in divine things. His work was merely to prepare the way for a higher teacher, by helping Gertrude to remove the hindrances that obstructed the path, and by holding her to a diligence in prayer. But, in the enlightening and guiding of her soul in the way of perfection, it was the Divine Spirit Himself who was her principal and proper Master.* He increased by His grace the propension of her soul towards God. Her patience, industry, and perseverance in the work of her perfection were wrought mainly by the concurrence of His support. He was ever with her, by His light, showing to her what to do or what to leave undone; what, and how, to amend in sins and defects, as also how to avoid their occasions. He thus prepared her for greater progress by removing from her all inordinate affection, clearing her soul from the clouds of passion, so that her natural reason, perfected by these means, was able better to discern good from evil. The intellectual faculties became also much more apt for receiving an access of supernatural light and help, so that in all points she was better fitted for advancing in her spiritual journey. His work with her was one of gradual development. Little by

* Father Faber, in his Growth in Holiness, says of the good spiritual director: "He does not lead his penitents; the Holy Ghost leads them. He is rather to go behind and to watch God going before."

See, also, a letter to a person of quality, by Father Surin, S.J., at the close of his Foundations of the Spiritual Life.

little she became better in the interior and exterior, and this was evident not only to her own sight, but also to that of others.

Her amendment, together with that of some few others that were in the same way, speedily, and it may be said suddenly, caused a great alteration for good in the house, both for exterior and interior. Many, who were not fit for those interior ways, yet began to look about them, and to pay more attention to perfection both within and without. And, in truth, it may be affirmed, partly on the ground of this experience, and partly for other reasons, that, in a convent of thirty or forty nuns, if three or four of good talent come to enter on an interior life, they will be the means of bringing the whole community, if out of order, to at least some external reasonable reformation. This they will be enabled to do by their sufferings and edifying demeanour, through the virtue of the Divine Spirit working in them, and sending His light out of them. To suppose the contrary, would be to suppose the rest of the Nuns destitute of all goodness and moral duty; qualities not often wanting, it is hoped, in professed Religious women. Now, had Gertrude, with her wit, added to the animosity and hardness of heart to which she had come, continued to decay in goodness, and to increase in evil habits and perverseness of will, she would doubtless have proved a most pernicious member of her community, and a corrupter of others. Already she had begun in a measure to disturb the peace of the house by factiousness and disobedience, so that from a kind of foundress to it, she might have become a ruin and a pestilence. "The best thing corrupted becometh the worst."

Although the Holy Ghost gave to Gertrude a plentiful succour to help her to overcome herself, yet this succour was often devoid of all sensible sweetness. The frequency of her interior darknesses is the cause why she often, in her confessions, speaks of serving and loving God without comfort, and commends the being contented to live only with the light of faith, as sufficient and most secure. By this frequent mention it may be gathered that such was her own practice. It was only at the beginning of her course, that, from a certain incapacity, she found it necessary to use such ejaculations as she got out of books. She came in a short time to use others merely of her own framing, as suggested to her by her own nature or spirit, or by the Divine Spirit, which oftentimes she set down in writing for her help in time of more aridity. Some others in the house liked them so well, that they copied them out, and in time a great store of these amorous affections of her collection, or framing, were to be found scattered here and there in divers books and papers. The second and third part of a book called the "Idiot's Devotions," contains these aspirations, Father Baker having collected them together, and rendered them into some order.

Her love of recollection was the chief cause that the fathers changed the time of mental prayer in the house, that it might be at a time more seasonable for her and others. The mental prayer was formerly at the end of Matins, at midnight, but, at her request, it was appointed to be at the end of Prime, in the morning. The mental prayer before supper was by her means much better observed. At her instigation, a Constitution was made which forbade the omitting of the mental prayer on recreation days or other occasions, a thing that formerly had often been the case. Such was Gertrude's love of mental prayer, and this mental prayer in her case was the seeking of God in her interior, there to pay Him her homage. God being a Spirit, is best sought after by the spirit of man, abstracted from the images of creatures. No doubt, for those who cannot make interior spiritual prayer, that mental prayer which uses the imagination and discourse, for the moving of the will towards God, is very profitable. Indeed, it is advisable for all to begin with this sort of meditation, or else to use immediate acts of the will and aspirations of love, made with effort. Those who cannot help themselves to mental prayer by the above methods are unfitted for its exercise, and must content themselves with vocal prayers or ejaculations, which, being transitory, never produce a lasting light in the interior. The internal light, with which Gertrude was favoured through means of her recollection and spiritual prayer, was no unfruitful thing. By the said light, besides the knowledge she obtained for the ordering of things concerning herself, she had very frequently, either by her cleared and elevated natural reason, or by a wholly supernatural light from God, a kind of sight or contemplation of the total dependance of herself and all other creatures whatsoever on

God, of the unrestricted absoluteness of His nature, and of the hanging of all things on His mere will. These contemplations were the ground of her humiliation and reformation.

Such a knowledge and conviction are the solid basis of a perfect humility, subjection, and obedience, whether to God or to others for God's sake, so that she says in her writings, "that the thought of God so ordaining it, would make her subject herself even to a worm." Of this humility she was wont to say, upon occasions, that none is able to conceive what it truly is by the powers of the natural reason. It can only be learned through the experience and contemplation of it, by conversation with God in internal prayer. Nothing can form in the soul this true and perfect humility, but the knowledge had from God by means of the grace of contemplation. None stood more in need of this powerful and only means for her thorough reformation than Gertrude More. She had great talents, and she knew it. She was in consequence exceedingly attached to her own judgment and will. Very stout-stomached she was, to use a homely phrase, though her external carriage was always seemly and correct. Such a spirit nothing was likely to humble and bring down but the consideration of God, and her utter dependence on Him. This knowledge is not to be got by books or by any external teaching, but is impressed on the soul by the touch of God in spiritual prayer. It is the sight of the infiniteness of God given to the soul by His own light, that alone can perfectly humble her. Till she has experienced this, she never can even know what perfect humility is, and much less be truly and perfectly humble. Gertrude's knowledge, therefore, before she came to the way of spiritual prayer, had but puffed her up. It was but a natural kind of knowledge, and led to the increase of pride, wilfulness, and disobedience. When she came to practise recollection, and the contemplation of the heavenly light, her high thoughts of her own wit and judgment vanished away.

All things formerly turned in her to the increase of pride, impatience, self-love, and other inordinations of soul. One particular example will suffice to show this. Her Abbess, out of judgment and discretion, noting the quality of her spirit, and seeing she stood in need of humiliation, made not much of her, showing her no particular mark of affection or esteem, but only treating her with kindness and respect. She expected more, and, not getting it, was wonderfully averted from her Abbess, and, hating to be subject to her, strove to set up against her a faction of disobedience and opposition. On the other hand, her Mistress, who had her under her charge about two years, made much of her, thinking to do her good that way: but this also turned as much to her hurt and to the increase of wilfulness and pride. The upshot of all was, that as she herself says, her heart grew as hard as a stone in regard to God and good things; whereas, before she came into Religion, though not very devout, she at least kept a good conscience, and was gentle and tractable. The knowledge of God, however, at her conversion, came to rectify her understanding, and soften her will. It brought her to know God, herself, her superiors, and others, according to the order of justice and truth. She thereby saw what her will was of itself, and what it by right should be; and she at once set about the changing of her life. Her amendment, together with that of some others, that were formerly in the same course, brought the house to a good peaceable state. Mr. More, Gertrude's father, coming to the convent again, as he passed that way from Antwerp to Paris, stayed there some days. It was the Easter next after that his daughter had entered upon her new spiritual course. He conversed some time with her and others at the grate during his stay, and, being an intelligent man, was not slow to observe a marked alteration for good, both in her and some others. He went away extremely well satisfied, which he had not been after his former visit. The same satisfaction he had again, upon his coming there the Michælmas following, as he passed by that way, returning from Paris to Antwerp. This was his last visit to Gertrude; for, having remained the winter following at Antwerp, in the spring he went to England, and never crossed the sea any more.

CHAPTER V.

FURTHER EXPLANATION OF THE APTITUDE FOR AN INTERIOR LIFE.—THE OFFICE OF AN EXTERNAL GUIDE.

Some readers would desire perhaps to have a further explanation of what has been called a thirst for God, or a propension towards Him. This foresaid propension, or thirst, is, in a manner, to be found in all men. It is a yearning for that infinite good which alone can satisfy; a sort of internal feeling after God, the heart groaning and labouring with a sense of want, yet not clearly knowing how to obtain its satisfaction. This propension is the primary root of all our spiritual good. In its naked self, and apart from grace, it is but natural, and is to be found in infidels, heathens, and heretics, especially the real Puritans. But they, wanting the light of faith, the grace of God, and spiritual instructions, which are only to be had in the Catholic Church, through ignorance and want of grace are unable to prosecute the work to which it moves them. It never therefore serves to bring them to felicity, or to a full satisfaction in soul, towards which yet it naturally tends, or invites. But true believing Christians may, by its being in them, animated with grace, and by their having other helps, much more easily work their way to a consummate happiness of soul. However, it must be said, that the measure of its consummation depends very much on the bodily temperament of each one.* All cannot attain the same perfection so rapidly, or so easily;

---

* "In the kingdom of grace, the law, which has the fewest exceptions, is that one, according to which the supernatural virtues are grounded on natural qualities."—Faber, Bethlehem, p. 253.

"There is something congenial between nature and grace. Hence it is that certain forms of holiness come almost natural to a man, suit his disposition, elicit the excellences of his individual character, and transform his nature rather than supplant it."—Faber's Conferences. Self-deceit ii.

"La nature lui avait donné tous les avantages de l'esprit. Elle avait l'esprit bon, le jugement très solide, un courage et une grandeur d'âme extraordinaires, toutes les dispositions naturelles, qu'on demande pour le recueillement interieur, et pour l'oraison."—Surin's Letters, No. 129.

See also Ruisbroek, De Verâ Contemplatione, 68.

some, on account of defects in bodily temperament, will be very much hindered in their efforts to find and enjoy God in their interior; at least without some very extraordinary grace, no less a one than the absolute alteration of their natural temperament, a grace rarely, if ever, given. Persons, therefore, of a very melancholy disposition, or who are naturally subject to violent passions, and so are unquiet in their nature, will find themselves very unapt for interior prayer, though they may have a great thirst after God. On the contrary, those that are of a sanguine temperament, that are merry and hearty, and of a quiet nature, may much more easily fit themselves for internal prayer, and contemplate God within themselves. Such was the temperament and bodily constitution of Gertrude More, descended to her from her father, probably; for her father was of this same temperament, but her mother not.

Behold, then, what great advantages she had, both exterior and interior, for the following out of a true spiritual course. She had, as a primary root, a strong propension to love God above all things. She had a bodily temperament naturally adapted for such a work, and external instructions also how to tend to the discovery and exercise of herself in the interior. Through these means and prayer she sought the gift of the internal guidance and conduct of the Divine Spirit, which she carefully observed, corresponded to, and followed, when vouchsafed. She had the light of the true faith, the help of that grace that alone makes a soul pleasing to God. She was in a Religious Order, where, in inclosure, she found all manner of external helps, superiors having ordered times and all other matters in the best manner for the exercise of contemplation, or a tendency to it, as the nature of the Order required. She also had the examples, encouragement, society, and concurrence of other good souls in the house, following the same spiritual course as herself, an advantage of no small moment. She, moreover, had bodily health and ability, which, though not great, were yet sufficient for the business of seeking after God in her interior. These endured till her last sickness, and then God supplied in spirit what was wanting to her in body, even to her happy death. When she had advanced somewhat in her spiritual course, her road became ever clearer and more plain, by the abundance of internal light. She therefore desired to forget all creatures, and attend to that one thing, which she was justly wont to term her "*All in All.*" When her contemplation of Him, according to the manner of this life, was consummated, she had but to pass immediately into another state of contemplation of more stability, security, and perpetuity, namely, the real sight and fruition of what before she had seen only as it were in a mirror, by a parable, and in hope. As sight, regard, and knowledge of God was the cause and worker of her humility, so was it likewise of an obedience to God, and to all others, where it was due, for Him. This is that obedience she speaks of so often in her writings. It consisted in this, that for God, and out of love and obedience to Him, she did willingly and easily those things which by any title it was her duty to do; obeying her superiors, and even all others, in reason, with great facility. Where it was her duty to abstain from anything, through regard to Him, she abstained; and for His sake she endured all the difficulties that fell upon her, external and internal. Her inward trials were great, such as internal desolations, contradictions of her strong will, and others of the like nature, which she bore with cheerfulness and alacrity. For matters external, there were seeming unkindnesses to digest, and neglects at the hands of others, as also her taking in good part her bodily infirmities, which were great. The regard of God made her to look on all these things, and on all the things of this life, and all, in fine, to be done or suffered in it, as mere trifles and nothings, save so far as they help or hinder the love and service of God, and the attaining of eternal happiness. Thither all her ambition turned, and the great longings of her soul. The sight of God, which she never actually and clearly enjoyed but in the times of set recollections, made her then to annihilate herself before Him. When the seasons of actual contemplation were past, she strove still to live in their virtue, through the impression they had wrought on her soul, so far as her frailty would permit. "O happy are those who are of such a temperament as to be able almost impetuously to concur with the divine grace. Nature and grace in them do, as it were in the current of one stream, unitedly flow towards God, whereas they who want the said qualities of temperament must laboriously work against the stream of nature.

But even in those who have the requisite temperament, the time for its being ripe for the work is in some sooner than in others. It is likely that in Gertrude it was not come to any ripeness or perfection in her younger years, or her movement towards God was overwhelmed by the natural affection she had to friends and kindred who surrounded her, she being of so affectionate a temper. Children, too, are fonder, generally, of the sports and pastimes of this life than of the things of the future. When these external impediments of living with her kindred, &c., were removed by her leaving home for a far country, then appeared in its full force the propension she had towards God, no longer choked by these hindrances to its development.

When God calls a soul to Religion, especially in a contemplative order, it is that this soul may be at perfect liberty to follow the attraction she has towards union with Him, by hearkening for His divine voice and inspirations, and by faithfully obeying them. For the obtaining of this end the Religious state has very many advantages. Its external discipline is so framed as to enable the soul much better to observe the interior divine motions and drawings. These are to be the stem and ground-work of all her doings, interior or exterior. She has also here the assistance of the Superior, or his substitutes, to prepare her by some general instructions for the observing and distinguishing the divine calls. It is his office to form a judgment and determination as to whether what the soul esteems to be a call from God is truly so, and to distinguish the drawings of God from those that are but natural or diabolical.* It is with this intention that Holy Church has given validity to Religious solemn profession. It is not, however, right for a Superior to try, as it were, to domineer over the drawings of the Holy Ghost, or to despise them. This certain persons run a danger of doing, who imagine themselves spiritual, but whose spirituality consists for the most part in exercises of the

---

* See Lallemant's *Spiritual Doctrine*, Principle iv., on the Guidance of the Holy Spirit, where he shews that docility to this interior guidance is not destructive of the obedience due to Superiors, nor to the recourse had by the soul to a spiritual director.

imagination.* They would wish to conduct all souls on their own road. But exercises that are properly and truly spiritual, are founded upon the lights and motions of the intellective not the sensitive soul, this latter working principally by the imagination, which is of little use in exercises truly spiritual. The Blessed John de Cruce, in his treatise entitled *Flammes d'amour*, vehemently reprehends some superiors and directors in his days, as faulty in the said point, namely, of diverting souls from observing and following the divine drawings, and of obliging them to follow their own ways and conceits. However, even in this case, it is the duty of the soul to subject herself to her superiors, leaving it to God one day to correct their error.

* Those who meditate only are very destitute of that supernatural light, which is the first principle of all spirituality.—*Surin's Foundations of the Spiritual Life*, B. iv. ch. ii. See also B. iii. ch. vi.

CHAPTER VI.

DIFFERENT KINDS OF PRAYER FOR BEGINNERS;
VOCAL PRAYER, MEDITATION, INTERIOR ACTS.

In order now to give the reader a clearer notion of the method of prayer practised by Gertrude More, it will be necessary here to give a more detailed account of the different kinds of prayer, usually practised by beginners, to attain to contemplation, which is the perfection of prayer. There are four kinds of prayer which souls begin with, led either by their aptness for some one of them, by the instinct of the Divine Spirit, or by the advice of their directors. Sometimes they begin with one of the four, being an inferior sort of prayer, and pass into another of them of a higher degree; and after that, when they are ripe for it, into contemplation.

The first of these four is vocal prayer. This is proper for the simple and unlearned, who are not apt for discursive prayer, as not having been educated in scholastic inventions and reasonings, though otherwise of sufficient natural abilities. This commonly is the case of women, lay brethren, and such like. Such prayer is proper for those who are not able to raise affections towards God by discourse, but are, as it were, totally drawn to the immediate exercise of the will. Now the probable reason why persons are drawn to this immediate exercise of the will, is that they have already a strong natural propension towards God. Their will being already sufficiently affected by grace, they do not require to raise their affections by reasonings. They feel, therefore, a disgust at all laboured reasonings or inferrings, which serve in this affair only for raising the affections. Vocal prayer, as a beginning, may serve those also who are learned, and who have in them ability for discourse, for the raising or bettering of their affections towards God. For such persons, though vocal prayers be good, and perhaps, strictly speaking, sufficient, yet, according to the need they have thereof, or the good they find therein, they will do well to promote their devotion, and increase their affection towards God, by discourse, reasoning or induction;—things which the understanding works by means of the imagination. And indeed, in the olden time, and even in the best and holiest times, all manner of souls began their course with vocal prayer, whether they had or had not in them ability for discourse, and whatsoever kind of spirit they were of. That it was so we see by ancient writers, who speak of no other kind of prayer until they come to contemplation, but only of the vocal prayer of the psalter, which they said all over once a day, and perhaps even more than once; such prayer served their turn, without seeking further help or instruction, until they attained to contemplation. This contemplation is a kind of prayer purely internal, without either words or reasoning. The power to make it comes from the divine assistance and inspiration; after being exercised some time, it becomes a habit. Persons who have come to contemplation may, perhaps, still continue vocal prayer, but they perform it now in a more spiritual manner. They exercise towards God a spiritual attention, with little or no use of imagination; whereas before they came to contemplation they proceeded with some grosser sensible images. These are now gone away or transcended; or, at least, not needed for prayer, for God is more spiritually apprehended. But in those ancient times they had other great helps, which were the cause why such vocal prayers proved so efficacious to them. These helps were, perfect solitude, silence, abstraction, utter separation from the world, and all worldly conversation, a freedom from all solicitudes of the world, with great bodily mortifications, such as fasting and abstinences, very great hardness of lodging, scarcity of sleep, coarseness and poverty in clothes, extremes of cold and heat, with other austerities and mortifications, taken on them by internal divine inspirations, or imposed by superiors or necessity. Their great seriousness, also, in their exercise of obedience, humility, patience, charity and other virtues, which is made mention of in the lives of the old Fathers, and of divers other Saints in ages since, was a help of some moment to them.

In their vocal prayers, however, or in any other prayer or exercise of their own, they were not to cling pertinaciously to this or that, but were to obey the interior drawing of the Divine Spirit, whose office it is to draw the soul in her exercises more and more towards Himself, causing them to become more and more spiritual. Nor is it any marvel that, using those helps, they attained so speedily to contemplation and perfection. And if we, in these ages, did the like, we should prevail as they did. But in these later ages, the most part, even of those souls that have a great propension and call towards God, never think to undertake those matters, which the ancients added to their vocal prayers. This may be either from the want of the like ability of body, or from lack of equal grace and call from God, or from some other defect not easy to discover. Certain it is, our bodies require far greater indulgences in meats and drinks, recreations and cessations, than theirs.

We find ourselves unable to be so continually attent on spiritual matters as they were; and other defects there are in us which were not in these ancient spiritual Fathers. Vocal prayer alone, therefore, is not enough for us as a groundwork, but we must add to it purely mental exercises. During these the soul may become recollected, and efficaciously exercise herself towards God, in amends and supply for the distractions in which she lives the rest of the day. These exercises must be continued till at all times, even the times of external employments, we are able with facility to raise our souls towards God.

In the case of Gertrude More, no amount of vocal prayer served to bring her to a spirit of recollection. After her conversion, however, she had the grace to be recollected even in the midst of continual business, conversations, and other extroversions, so that these things did her no harm, being only a needful recreation to her spirit. When she went to her recollection, her propension and call towards God, in the fund of her soul, was so potent and vehement, that she could immediately converse with God: all sensible images of matters formerly handled by her, and of all other things, being abandoned and brushed away.

In cases, however, where vocal prayer, together with the exercise of virtue, suffices to promote contemplation, there is no road easier, readier, or securer than it; none less perilous to head or health, less subject to diabolical illusions, or to indiscretion in the use of it. And in time, in a capable soul, vocal prayer becomes spiritualized, as it did in Gertrude More, by whom the Divine Office, in time, came to be performed in a state of recollection, and in much gust and light of soul. She herself thus speaks of it in her book of confessions:

"The Divine Office is such a heavenly thing, that in it we find whatsoever we can desire. For sometimes in it we address ourselves to Thee for help and pardon for our sins; and sometimes Thou speakest to us: so that it pierceth and woundeth with desire of Thee the very bottom of our souls. Sometimes, again, Thou givest a soul to understand more in it of the knowledge of Thee, and of herself, than ever could, by any teaching in the world, have been made known to it in five hundred years; Thy words are works."

By this it appears plain, that her recollections in the performance of the Divine Office had some extraordinary light and favours from God. So far, then, with regard to vocal prayer. Gertrude had studied Latin, that she might more profitably recite her Breviary.

Another sort of prayer for beginners is discursive prayer, which we commonly call meditation. And this is very good for them that need it, and can perform it. Some need it not because they are able to exercise the will, immediately, and without discourse, especially after they have some time used discourse. This is the case of them that have in the will a strong propension towards God; for these are either, from the commencement, utterly unable by any discourse to raise affections to God, (which was the case with Gertrude More,) or else, if they be able to discourse and need it, yet such ability and need lasts not long. And why not? Because they have scarce begun to meditate when they find themselves ripe for the exercise of the will, either by way of immediate acts, or of ejaculations, natural or forced. At the commencement of her course, this last was the method used by Gertrude More. Those who are blessed with a good propension towards God, when they meditate or discourse, do it not with any violence of effort, nor with any great industry, nor sifting long the matter of the meditation by curious reasonings; but presently upon the imagination of the point, they fall into the use of the will, and so spend the greatest part of their exercise. They do this chiefly through the virtue of this strong propension towards God, which disables them indeed for discourse, but amply makes up for its loss.

Through its virtue the soul is enabled to do immediately, by the will, what those that want it can only attain, less efficaciously, by means of discourse moving the will. The business of meditation is to find out, and reflect on, the motives men have to love God and their neighbour. The consideration of these motives helps to rouse the will into life. The principal part, however, of meditation, is in the understanding, the end of it in the will. The memory, imagination, and other rational powers, are called to busy themselves with activity, not for the sake of their own satisfaction, but that, the understanding being thus enlightened, the will may be more easily moved, whether to love and works of piety towards God, or to good works towards the neighbour.

But God is gracious, and to those who persevere doing what they can by meditation, He gives occasionally, at least, short gusts of contemplation, lifting them up for a brief interval into the clear, unclouded sphere of the spirit. Some, also, go forward from the exercises of meditation, to a kind of prayer more advanced and spiritual, abstracted from all images and discourse. Gertrude More never could make meditation. Women generally are less capable of meditation, which is such a task for the reasoning powers.

A third sort of prayer for beginners is the exercise of immediate acts—*immediate*, because the soul by them treats with God immediately, i.e., without the medium of discourse, reasoning, inferring, or deducing. This sort of prayer is performed by the will of the superior soul, but not without the use of the imagination and understanding. The understanding must necessarily use, in forming the act, some sensible conception of the thing to be willed, presented to it by the imaginative power. There is, however, no formal discourse or reasoning. There is, by the understanding only, an apprehension, and without further study an act is elicited by the will. An act thus produced from a prepared will, already leaning towards God, has in it more force and power than one produced by dint of reasonings from a sluggish and laggard will. A ready will does not require to search laboriously by meditation for reasons and motives. The act, therefore, which it produces, is not only made with far more efficacy, but also with more promptitude and facility, and far less industry. So that the head and mental powers are less wearied, and in less peril of receiving harm by such exercise. The reason why some prosper so well without formal meditation, may be gathered from what has been said above, the readiness of the will supplying the lack of discourse.

Meditation, however, may be used at the commencement of their course by souls best disposed for internal prayer; but they will not tarry long in it, that is to say, not many years, and some not many months, and some not many weeks, but will pass from such meditation into immediate acts. Sometimes, perhaps, for a little while they may be driven to reassume meditation, but they will always perform it with less turmoil of the understanding, and more activity of the will, than is the case of those who are not naturally disposed for internal ways.

With regard to the immediate acts treated of, the subject of them may be anything that has reference to the love of God, or the neighbour, such as acts of resignation, patience, obedience, humility, sorrow for sin, purposes of amendment, or the avoiding of sin, the doing offices of Christian charity, &c.

These the soul undertakes for God's sake. Other acts the soul raises towards God, without relation to herself, as when the act is one congratulating God that He is what He is, and wishing that all should serve and love Him, with other acts of benevolence or well wishing to God.

Such acts are to be accounted immediate acts, and not be esteemed exercises of contemplation, for they are done with some force of the will, election of the matter, and industry of the person making them, together with much and necessary use of the imagination. But there is nothing of this sort in contemplation. In contemplation the aspirations are those of the spirit, entirely abstracted from the imagination and other rational powers. These elevations of the will of the superior soul, have their root in its natural propension towards God. When the soul is in a state of grace, they become habitual in those that have entered on an internal life. They have then also a freedom and a vigour, which, unaided, they could never attain.

Indeed, it is the Divine Spirit in such souls who, intimately inhabiting them, is in them the primary worker and spring of all. When He moves, they move in concert with Him, and their movement is more His than theirs, but both are so intimately blended together, that the movement of the soul is sometimes as it were lost in His. She is never, however, really passive, though at times she seems so.

It has already been said that Gertrude More was altogether incapable of meditation. She was equally unable to do herself any good by the exercise of immediate acts, last treated of. This was probably because, in forming these acts, it is necessary to use the imagination as a starting point; whereas her soul tended rather to direct acts of love grounded upon no formal motive, but proceeding straight to God from the affectionateness of her heart towards Him. This kind of prayer is the fourth of those that are proper for beginners. Before, however, proceeding to its consideration, it will be well to examine more closely still the nature of that propension towards God, with which this affectionateness of heart is intimately connected, and which was so strong in Gertrude More.

There is in all men, in all souls, a natural yearning after God, which is indelible, and must remain everlastingly, even in the souls of the damned in hell. But the aptitude for leading an interior life is not to be found in all.

This aptitude probably depends very much on the qualities of the bodily temperament and mental character.

In some persons these are more, in others less, favourable to the cultivation of a recollected spirit, and in such proportion the aptitude for leading an interior life is greater or less. None are altogether inapt, few have the aptitude in a high degree. Of those that have it in a good measure, fewer still attain that interior spirit for which they are naturally fitted. Some fail of this for want of seeking the divine grace, many being heathens, heretics, and other infidels; others fail by living, through their own fault, in mortal sin; others, again, through want of opportunity and a commodious state of life.

And of those that are in a state in which there is a commodity for seeking God in their interior, some want instructions how to proceed, others are so plunged and rooted in the habits of sin, that they will not better themselves, or strive to co-operate with the divine grace, which is ever ready to help them. Those, however, who have an aptitude for an internal life, and set about seriously to seek God in their interior, easily come to find and enjoy Him, even though before they have a long time together lived in the habits of great mortal sins; and much more easily may they, whose propension has not been corrupted through ill-living, but who have lived harmless and innocent lives. At the outset, however, of an interior life, the soul is not able to work with vigour or facility, because the images of creatures, caused by inordinate affections to them, yet cling to her. The affections, with the images caused by them, being by proper exercises expelled, then the soul comes to work easily, freely, and potently. She comes, in fact, to the state called contemplation, which consists of upward motions, caused and raised by grace working upon the natural propension of the soul towards God.

Before this state, however, can be attained, the bad images must be expelled by means of good ones. This being done, the good ones will not hinder the working of the spirit, but will yield and give place to it; for, before the spirit can work, it must first have all sensible images, both good and bad, removed. So the beginner, in a spiritual cause, begins with the use of images that are good ones; for it is impossible to begin a spiritual course with the exercises of the spirit. And so with St. Paul, (1 Corinth. xv.) "Not that which is spiritual, must be first, but that which is sensible; afterwards that which is spiritual." Of the same meaning are the words of St. Bernard, that "miraculous is the contemplation that is not founded upon meditation precedent;" where by meditation he means any good exercises with the use of sensible images. Now, in these four sorts of prayer which pertain to beginners, the work is done partly by the soul's rational powers. Through them she seeks to become acquainted with God and divine things by consideration, with the use of sensible images. In such exercises, they that have no natural drawing to the interior life, must abide while they live. This they will do, both profitably to themselves and others, as also agreeably to God, it being the good active life.

But those that have in them the nobler drawing to the interior, after due prosecution of these lower exercises, pass to those that are purely spiritual, not depending on the imagination at all, but consisting merely in the spiritual elevation of the will.

The aspirations thus made are formless, having no particular or definite shape; they are but the uprisings of the human spirit, longing for union with the Spirit of God.

They proceed from a habit of good affection in the superior soul, got by means of the precedent exercises. This habit brings back to the soul, in a measure, the ability she had in the state of innocence, when she had no inordinate images hindering or troubling her in her workings towards God.

CHAPTER VII.

PRAYER OF SENSIBLE AFFECTIONS.—
CONTEMPLATION.

The fourth sort of prayer proper for beginners, is the prayer of sensible affection; *sensible*, because chiefly in the senses of the bodily nature; *of affection*, because it consists in the will and love, rather than in the understanding.

Now, there are some temperaments naturally more affectionate than others; these can easily exercise such their affections towards God, in, and by their corporal nature, and that without seeking any reason for it. Persons of this character, that have so much affection in them, and are religiously disposed, desire to find an exercise for it some way or other towards God.

But though they have the natural habit of it in themselves, they do not always know how to make use of this habit in act, for one of these two reasons; either because to make acts of love to God is a thing quite new to them, or because through indisposition of body they are disinclined for so doing. The weather, or other secret natural causes, often greatly indispose persons of this temperament; and at those times these affectionate souls are in great obscurity, aridity, and distress, not being able to help themselves with any discourse. This was very frequently the case with Gertrude More. But how, and with what exercises are they to help themselves at the first?

They may do as Gertrude did, by gathering out of books proper patterns for the exercise of sensible devotion and affection, or they may use such aspirations as shall suggest themselves to them; the like for instance as, O my Lord God, when shall I love Thee as Thou deservest to be loved? Oh, that I were freed from myself, that I might love Thee! When shall I be united to Thee? When shall I love Thee with all my heart and all my soul? In a thousand such like ways, proper and suitable to her affection, may the soul exercise herself, either taking the affections out of books, or, what is better, using what are suggested to her by her own nature. But those suggestions are of the sensuality, and are sensible, not spiritual, aspirations. Nevertheless, this sensual exercise of affection is, in our corrupted nature, absolutely necessary as a foundation, before the soul can attain to an exercise that shall be truly spiritual. In times of bodily indisposition, when neither nature suggests, nor yet concurs to their exercise, these souls must still use and produce these affections, though there be not any gust in them, nor light by them; if, that is, they cannot see how otherwise to do better. God will accept of their good will, and promote their souls by means of this exercise in such manner as He best knows how. Accordingly, Gertrude More, when affected with bodily indisposition and obscurity, never desisted on this account from doing what she could, and sought to be patient and resigned for what she could not do. She was always careful still to observe her times of recollection, and do whatever grace and nature would enable her to do. By so doing she gained as much, if not more, by darkness and indisposition, as by clearer light and more sensible devotion; for she got light and knowledge what to do, and good will and grace to perform it; and what more was there to be wished for? Now, it must be remarked, that there is a great difference in this prayer of sensible affection, between those who have a propension to the interior, and those who have not. In those who have an aptitude for interior ways, it tends much more freely towards the spirit, so that they enjoy a measure of internal light, as having their soul somewhat, though not perfectly, abstracted from the lower nature. In this light they see their interior and the state of it; though their exercise has its root yet in the sensitive nature, and their affections proceed principally from the fleshy heart.

The same thing is to be said of their meditation. Those who have not the aptitude for the interior in their exercises of sensible affection, remain plunged in sensuality, the soul being much obscured and little capable of divine light, or the motions of the Spirit.

There is need of discretion in the exercise of sensible affection, as, by yielding over much to tears and the like, great harm may be done to the head and health, and other impediments of spirit may arise. The internal light serves to guide those who have an aptitude for it, and teaches them discretion in this matter. But others, wanting this spiritual light, have the more need to help themselves by natural reason, taking heed they do not hurt themselves by yielding too much to sensible devotion, when they enjoy it in any fulness.

Their excess, however, is not likely to be so hurtful to them as it would be to those internally disposed.

Gertrude persisted in this prayer of affections, until from the sensitive nature they had penetrated within, and become spiritual aspirations, so as to be truly acts of contemplation. This contemplation increased in spirituality until her death, by a higher elevation of soul, and a more and more perfect abstraction. As these acts of sensible affection penetrate the spirit, and become spiritual, so also does vocal prayer, with the use of mortifications. But it is not probable that ever any one passes out of meditation immediately into contemplation. It is likely that first his meditation ceases, and then he uses immediate acts, till he attains to contemplation.

The contemplation that follows all these four sorts of exercises is alike, that is, it is mainly in the will, without the exercise of the imagination. But some persons rise to a higher elevation than others, according to the measure of grace, and their diligence in the use of it; and according to the measure of mortification the soul has attained. This mortification is attained either by mortifications of God's immediate sending, or through His permission, by the means of creatures. The speediness of arriving at contemplation, however, principally depends upon the measure of the soul's propension towards God. It was very great and potent in Gertrude. Grace made her to undergo with sweetest patience the mortifications which frequently fell on her. She was quiet by nature, too. Her passions were not so violent, but that she could easily hold them in, at least from exterior disorderly behaviour. Those who have an equal thirst for God, but are more unquiet in their natures, and have less power over their passions, will probably be longer ere they attain to contemplation.

In this exercise of sensible affections Gertrude did not tie herself strictly to any method. She sometimes made the affections mentally only, at other times vocally also, according to what best befitted the disposition of the moment, or to what her nature or spirit drew her, and what most promoted her way towards God.

Though of the sorts of prayer for beginners, Gertrude could employ only the fourth, yet others may perhaps profitably use two, three, or all of the four. The selfsame person may have occasion to use such variety, for there is no certain rule or limit. The soul must observe herself what is her call, and what most fits her, and what she is most drawn to; and then, with serious pursuit of her mental prayer, one way or other, she will not fail to make profit in her prayer. In treating with Gertrude More, all that Father Baker did was to advise her one way or other to perform her mental prayer, and not to give it up either for aridity, obscurity, or other difficulty. He told her also, since none of the three first sorts suited her, she should betake herself to the fourth, in such a manner as experience should show her to be best. When the soul has got, by means of mental prayer, into her interior, she must observe the divine admonitions and drawings, and not cling pertinaciously to any of her spiritual exercises or other doings, by reason of opinion or custom, or of what she has heard, or read in books, or what she has at other times experienced. It is of the highest moment that she should well observe this point. For sometimes it happens that the soul fixes herself too pertinaciously to one sort of prayer, when she should betake herself to some other. Whereas she ought to hold herself in readiness at once to leave any or all of the lower sorts of prayer, so as to betake her to contemplation, when it is fitting time.

These directions are for those souls principally who feel drawn to an interior life, and who are found to have sufficient judgment and abilities to discern the attractions of the Spirit of God. For by the internal light they will be able to distinguish what is the best for them, and whither God would lead them.

There is another defect in the pursuance of an interior life, in all respects equally hurtful with the above-mentioned defect about the manner of prayer, and that is in the matter of mortification.

A spiritual life consists of these two things, prayer and mortification. Now, the one being altogether insufficient without the other, a good course must be held, both by the director and the soul herself, in the matter of mortification, as well as in the matter of prayer. And such course is not always well held, to the great damage of those souls that are in the way of contemplation. The defect lies in this, that in matters of mortification that have no obligation one way other by any law, divine or human, the soul does not do according to what her call is. She acts in them rather according to opinion or custom, to what she has read in books, conceived by her natural reason, heard from others, heretofore practised herself, or seen others to practise. But none of these respects are to be regarded by a contemplative liver, in things which are not sinful or defective, but only of that sort that are called indifferent. As touching them, she is to do them or leave them undone, according as she finds them to be profitable or hurtful to her, thus attending to her call.

In the point of mortification, Gertrude followed these three rules; first, that she should do all that she was required to do by any law, divine or human. In this was comprised her obedience to all divine injunctions, not only in matters of obligation, but also in things indifferent, for the divine inspiration is a principal law to a spiritual liver. Secondly, that she should forbear and abstain from all things that she was bound to forbear and abstain from, either by the above-mentioned laws, or by divine inspiration. Thirdly, that she should undergo and suffer, with the best patience and resignation she could, all crosses and contradictions of her natural will, either in internal matters, such as aridities, obscurities, temptations, griefs, &c.; or in bodily pains, difficulties, diseases, infirmities, &c.; or in the matters of honour, fame, and estimation, such as disgraces, unkindnesses, neglects, and the like; or in the loss of friends, or in want of necessaries and contentments for the body.

These crosses she must suffer patiently, whether they shall come immediately on her from God, or by the means of creatures. These mortifications were enough for her. But though a spiritual life consists of prayer and mortification, and neither of them without the other is sufficient, yet of the two prayer is the principal and the nobler part, as being the end of mortification, and as being that which in this business is sought for, for itself. Mortification is sought for only to enable the soul to pray well; in which well praying consists the happiness of this life, as the happiness of the future life consists in the prayers proper for that life. Mortification serves this end, because it batters, breaks, and kills the natural will, which is the only impediment of perfect prayer; and perfect prayer consists in contemplation, which is an actual union with God. Now, the doings, abstainings, and sufferings, whereto all mortification may be reduced, serve to break in pieces our own will, for we either do things repugnant to our natural will and to sensuality; or, if they be pleasing to our natural will, yet we do them not for the end sought by nature, which always is self, but for the conformity of our will to the will of God. Mortification, then, in itself and of itself, is not prayer, which is union of the soul with God. It is, however, commonly an effect of union past, or some disposition to a union future. Prayer has these further graces and virtues in it.

The first and principal is, the essential happiness of this life, which is the union of the soul with God in her three powers.

The second is, that by the means of prayer, which is conversation with God, who is all light, and the fountain of all light, the soul that was of herself in darkness, receives a light for her conduct in the spiritual life. This light, which may be termed a supernatural discretion, enables her to discern all that concerns her in the aforesaid three heads of mortification. By this light she is taught how to perform the things that belong to her of obligation, and how to behave herself about matters that are indifferent, and are not of obligation, whether to do them, or to abstain from them; how far, and in what manner, and to what end to do them; and all this with a final relation to God, His honour and will.

The third virtue of prayer, is that it gives grace and strength of will to perform those mortifications that are contrary in themselves, or in their ends, to the inclinations of corrupt nature; whereas, without such strength, the soul would remain weak, unwilling, and utterly unable for such a task. The fourth virtue, or grace of prayer, is that its very actual exercise is, of its own self, one of the greatest mortifications and destructions of the natural will; for, by the exercise of prayer, the soul gets out of herself and her condition of nature. By resignations, aspirations, elevations, and other exercises, she is raised to a spiritual condition, and in some sort becomes deified, as being altogether of one will with God. It is for these reasons that, in her writings, Dame Gertrude so much extols the virtue and the necessity of prayer. For the conduct of her soul, in the way of the spirit, she used to receive a great treasure of light by means of prayer. By this light she discerned that divers indifferent matters and practices, which she allowed herself, were no impediments to her, but rather necessary helps, considering the constitution of her body. She yielded, therefore, to them, not out of her natural delight in them, but out of obedience to God and His will, which was signified to her by the clear light of prayer. In yielding to things naturally pleasing to her, though she did so from a pure motive, yet, nevertheless, she doubtless was sometimes drawn by nature into blemishes and imperfections. These, however, at least in her next recollection, were purged away by God and in God, inasmuch as she had incurred them, not out of affection or with deliberation, but out of frailty or inadvertence, and upon occasions which she could not avoid, or which were, as it were, enjoined her by the said divine light and will.

SCHEME OF FATHER BAKER'S TEACHING ON DIVINE CALLS.

From an Appendix to Sancta Sophia.

In all our actions or omissions, in all occasions of doing something, or forbearing, or suffering, or receiving, whether from God or a creature, there are these conditions:

1. Either there is an exterior law commanding the thing or forbidding it, which is in all such occurrences to be esteemed an undoubted call of God. The exterior law is therefore to be faithfully kept, in the doing or forbearing of the thing occurring. The interior call is to be as faithfully kept, by doing or omitting the thing with the movement of the spirit of grace.

2. In actions which no law, human or divine, commands or forbids, if they are extraordinary, they are not to be practised without the sanction of exterior authority. The

interior call is, however, to be noted with esteem. In actions implying no inconvenience or notable singularity, the inward call is a sufficient guide, and ought to be carefully observed and obeyed, lest the soul, receiving God's graces in vain, be deservedly deprived of them.

CHAPTER VIII.

THE CALL OF GOD TO THE USE OF THINGS INDIFFERENT.—THE SOUL TO PROCEED GRADUALLY.

This holy Nun had naturally an active brain and a stirring imagination, which took great delight in feeding its faculties with whatsoever savoured of curiosity, novelty, or elegancy of wit. Such a disposition made her impatient and incapable of much solitude, silence, or abstraction; nay, it drove her, before her conversion, almost wholly to the contrary. And when she would give herself to solitude and abstraction, before she got into the way of true recollection, presently she found herself painfully molested with malicious thoughts, tending to much fear. These inconveniences made solitude and abstraction horrible to her, and caused her to desire to be much in company, talking, hearing, and speaking of news, and of curious and other delightful things. These amusements in themselves were not evil; indeed, at that time they were rather good for her, because they served to keep her from greater damage other ways. They could not, however, but be an occasion to her of incurring many imperfections, besides serving to the evil confirmation of her natural habits. But, being in Religion, and having a good will towards God, though as yet she had not found the way to practise it aright, she, in times that were proper for solitude in the house, occupied herself for the most part in reading. The books she read were either spiritual, or contained good or tolerable matter. Of this latter kind were those that treated of the sayings and doings of philosophers, and other wise men, and secular stories judiciously written. She left unread no spiritual book that she could come by (and great store she got of them.) She was delighted with such as were historical, and preferred good poetry to prose. She naturally loved rhyme, and being yet but four or five years old, she would make rhymes in conversing with her father, who was much delighted with her company, which, owing to her merry disposition, was a great recreation to him.

Du Bartus, the French writer, as translated

into English by Silvester, she was much delighted to read.

Perhaps neither the author nor the translator were as sound in their belief as they should have been. Yet the works in themselves are good, both as to matter and style; and she, whose belief was sound and perfect, took what was good, without getting any hurt by them. But novelties were so grateful to her, that having once read any book, she took no delight in a second reading. In such disposition of heart she read over all S. Gertrude's works. But books that were merely vain, or trivial, and contained no true virtue or wisdom in them, gave her no delight.

These readings, after her entry into Religion, were the greatest contentment she found therein, her state being then one of discontentment.

In this reading she occupied herself at those seasons when, by the order of the house, all were to be solitary and silent. At other times she would always be in company where she had the commodity of talking, at the grate or in the house, which for the time kept out of her head thoughts of discontentment, and other pernicious thoughts. This, I say, was her natural condition and carriage before she got into the way of recollection. In sum, her whole inclination was extroversion, and no kind of seeming disposition had she for introversion, or an internal life, to which there is not a greater enemy than such an imagination, and such other qualities of disposition as have been attributed to her above.

Nothing could have wrought the bringing of such a one into an internal life but the energy she had in her will, assisted with much grace and a good natural understanding, which enabled her to observe and pursue the divine internal lights and motions in the right way.

In this work of reformation, the Divine Spirit proceeded not violently, so as to oppress the bodily nature and destroy it. This is not His wont. He ever seeks, on the contrary, to bear it up in good plight, so that it may better serve the spirit. Sweetly and graciously He allures the soul, and, as it were, only extorts from her at first a giving up of her inordinate affections, whilst for the perfect reforming of the evil habits, He is content to tarry and expect, seeking to amend them by little and little. Such conduct does the Divine Spirit hold, as to those things which are in themselves sins or imperfections, which the soul out of frailty or inadvertence oftentimes incurs, rather than out of affection to them, or to their occasions. They are the result of ill habits formerly contracted, or of nature. In the same manner does the Spirit often deal with His disciple about things indifferent. He does not urge or admonish her to use them at first starting, in the most perfect manner, but to use them with some degree of perfection, as tending by little and little towards perfection. Perhaps He permits, yea, advises the soul to use them in no manner of perfection, save so far as that she shall do what she does, with respect to them, as upon obedience to His divine call and will. And this He does sometimes out of regard for the weakness of the soul's natural propension towards God, or for the small measure of grace added. At other times He permits and counsels the retaining of certain things, for the bearing up of the bodily nature, which would in many be destroyed, if they should go about suddenly, or, as it were, violently, to reform the sensuality by mortification in things of themselves indifferent. Of such sort are those matters of extroversion, to which Gertrude was much subject; to wit, conversation at the grate, or within the house, letters, hearing or speaking of news, curiosities, or other things.

Such things, of themselves, as they are not meritorious, so are they not sins; though oftentimes they are, through frailty, but not necessarily, the occasions of sin and imperfections. The reading of books, secular or profane, whose matter is not bad, though it be not spiritual, is not sin, nor a likely occasion of sin. Such use of indifferent things, though of itself less perfection than the contrary practice, yet may be, as in the case of Gertrude More, a necessary diversion of the mind for the time, and a recreation profitable for a well-dispositioned soul, as enabling her thereby to perform her future recollection with more vivacity.

For a soul that undertakes such diversions of the mind, not from deliberate affection, but as a necessary mode of unbending her spirit, will find no impediment by them. The Holy Spirit, then, so seems to have proceeded with His disciple Gertrude; amending little by little, and not over hastily or violently, those things which were defective or unlawful in her, and expecting patiently the time of a further reformation. Those indifferent things which were natural to her temperament, and habituated to her by custom, she still in great measure retained, yet with some abatement of her affection to them. She says in her writings: "I desire no consolation, but that I may be in solitude and silence all the days of my life, and be able to live without all consolation human or divine, no recreation by conversation, or other business and employment, but so far as it is necessary to bear up my spirit to attend to things more serious, and unto Thee, my God, at convenient times. Let all necessary distractions, by help of Thy grace, serve as a mere cessation, rather than that, by the least affection to them, or comfort in them, they should become as an impediment to my aspiring to Thee." And a little after she speaks thus of herself: "I who am not, without much and often diverting myself to indifferent things, able to attend to Thee in my soul at other times, and this by reason of my great weakness of body and of head. Let all this imperfection humble me, and let it be no impediment to my truly loving, serving, and praising Thee. To adhere wholly to Thee, is my only desire in all I do." These are her words in the said place.

By these words, and others in her writings, it is plain that when she did not mortify herself in indifferent things, it was not out of affection to them, but out of judgment and discretion; in order to be the better able by such recreation to perform her more serious business with God. In her recollections she saw plainly that the Divine Spirit did not only not reprehend her proceedings, but did approve them till His further grace should enable her to use those indifferent things in greater perfection.

But no man is judge in his own cause. Gertrude therefore had recourse to Father Baker, submitting to his judgment all those lights which she conceived to come from the Holy Ghost, ready to abide by his decision.

Father Baker upheld her, by his approval, in the way she acted with regard to the usage of these indifferent things, seeing in it God's will for her, through the clearness of the lights in her conscience.

Thus it is, that the following of the lights of the Holy Ghost in no way derogates from the subservience due to external directors, but rather furthers it. For the Holy Ghost Himself inspires His disciples to seek the security of external sanction.

CHAPTER IX.

TOO MUCH HASTE HURTFUL.—EXAMEN OF CONSCIENCE.—IN WHAT MANNER MADE BY CONTEMPLATIVE SOULS.

Cassian, in his Conferences, speaks very much about the manner of making good use of indifferent things, terming them *middle* things. He makes a threefold division of things, some are in themselves good, some bad, some *middle*. These middle, or indifferent things, take their character from the way in which they are used. They are good, if used for good, bad if used for evil.

These middle things are many, such as conversation at the grate, or anywhere else, reading, writing, exercise, or employments of the body, solicitudes, or cares of the mind, recreations, &c. All these things of themselves are middle, or indifferent. They neither merit nor demerit of themselves, that is, where there is no obligation to them; but the intention, actual or habitual, may make them meritorious, or demeritorious, profitable or unprofitable.

Now, the Divine Spirit in His conduct of a soul never inspires her to do or omit anything contrary to her obligations.

Whatever, therefore, Gertrude More did against her obligations, is to be attributed to her own natural will or judgment, and her miscarriage therein must be attributed to ignorance or frailty. And who, in this life, is not sullied with such errors and frailties?

But for indifferent things, not forbidden, though in themselves directly contrary to true introversion, yet because her natural temperament was wonderfully inclined to them, the Divine Spirit, by a light in her conscience, permitted them to her, teaching her, nevertheless, to purify her intention about them. In all this Gertrude had the approval of Father Baker. Had she been denied all extroversion, naturally it would have destroyed her bodily health, which was but weak. A stronger constitution could have endured more violence to nature, in the way of such mortification, but we must take hers as it was. The Divine Spirit gave her grace not only to do what she did with purer intention, but also to contract fewer and lesser sins or blemishes through so doing. And afterwards, in time of recollection, all was amended and supplied, through the virtue of her strong propension towards God. The Divine Spirit also taught her in process of time so to behave, with regard to these indifferent things, that they should be no impediment to her future recollection, but rather a preparative disposition for the same. And Gertrude found, by experience, that after she had spent the rest of the day in extroversions, her recollection notwithstanding proved so clear, that there scarcely remained any sensible image to hinder or trouble the immediate conversation and treaty of her soul with God.

The Divine Spirit thus accommodated His grace to her natural temperament, as is His wont, permitting things not evil, but yet seeking to reform in time, and by little and little, what was an impediment to profound recollection and perfection. He does not actually alter the natural temperament, but, by virtue of introversion and recollection, pacifies the passions as to their inordinate risings and desires. This He did gradually with Gertrude. In virtue of her deep recollections and introversions, she, in tract of time, and for a good space before her last sickness, was come to have the exorbitancies of her natural passions and rational powers very much, if not wholly, pacified. In her later days, through this divine work, she was grown to be very capable of solitude, internal and external, not only for the time of recollection, but also at other times. She could very well endure to be at all times alone, and to have no external solicitudes, or doings, further than external necessities required.

After meals, however, she found that conversation with others was necessary for her bodily health and for the refreshment of her spirit. Accordingly, out of judgment, more than out of affection to such recreations and extroversions, she yielded to them; for now she was become wholly God's, and affected and intended only Him.

The over-much vivacity of her natural powers was come to be taken away, and their excessive activity to be somewhat dulled by her profound introversions, for naturally her head would be always working. By the same means, probably, was accomplished in her what sound spiritual writers call the drawing of the external senses into the interior, and the internal into the fund or bottom of the soul.

Gertrude now gave herself to matters of extroversion with less adhesion, not pouring herself out upon them, as she had done in the forepart of her spiritual life. This grace she got by virtue of some contemplations she had given her of the vanity of all created things in themselves. Her recollections also sometimes so totally absorbed her affections into God, that she left them, as it were, firmly fixed in Him, and loosed from creatures. Such a state, however, she came to only by degrees, and for some time after her conversion there was outwardly but little change in her. Her extroversions continued the same as before, and it was as if she had had " the solicitude of all the Churches" upon her; nothing concerned the house, but her head or hand, or both of them, were in it.

None more conversed at the grate than she did, for the recreation of herself and others; none more conversant with all the news inside and outside of the house; none wrote more letters. She willingly took upon herself the office of Celleraria, by which she had more solicitude than all the rest of the house, unless it were the Abbess. And all this she did with a good intention to God, if not actual, at least virtual. When she had become more interior, she durst not much read spiritual books before the hour of recollection. This was partly because her spirit did not relish external instructions, and partly because the matters of them would have preoccupied her mind and made her less potent for her recollection.

Indeed, in order to divert herself from what was over-serious, she from time to time read some books, containing good or indifferent matters, and nothing hurtful, though not spiritual.

Now who, seeing these things in Gertrude More, and not well acquainted with her interior, and experienced in the manner of divine calls, would have imagined that she had any aptness for an internal life, or that instructions conducing to contemplation could be proper for her? How strange, and how far different are the ways and calls of the Divine Spirit in some souls from what they are in others.

Therefore, for the use of things indifferent, none is to be judged and condemned by others, especially no soul that in anywise seeks after God.

The Holy Father S. Benedict, in his Rule, gives very good counsels to the Abbot for the bearing with things yet imperfect. He bids him " take heed of breaking the vessel through seeking overmuch and indiscreetly to rub it, and do away the rust." He condemns overmuch violence and hastiness, but would have the rust taken away by a soft rubbing, and little by little, the vessel being so weak that it would not endure a hasty, speedy, and violent rubbing and cleaning.

In the same Chapter S. Benedict goes on to bid the Abbot to temper his doings, imitating the discretion of Jacob, who said : " If I make my sheep to labour overmuch in their journey, they will all die in one day :" " Let him so temper all things that the strong may desire them, and the infirm not fly from them."

Examination of conscience is rightly considered one of the main pillars of a spiritual building.

1. First, then, Gertrude exercised a continual care over herself, both within and without, all the day. She did this not anxiously,

or scrupulously, but "*timorate et suaviter,*" observing that counsel or precept of S. Benedict, "At all times to look to one's doings." This is no very difficult task in a contemplative Order, where there is not much distraction by active duties, more especially in a Convent of women. Those, therefore, that so live, have abundant commodity to have such a care of themselves; and few occasions of great falls, or deep plunges, which are commonly occasioned by manifold distractive business. All men know that it is better, by diligence, to eschew the committing of a fault, than being less diligent to have more occasion to inquire after faults committed, though it be for the amendment of them. The falls of contemplative livers are commonly so spiritual and subtle as hardly to be capable of being palpably discerned. These spiritual defects are best and most properly amended by spiritual means, that is to say, by elevating the spirit to God, by which it becomes cleansed from all the spiritual defects it has incurred; and they are amended even before they are known.

In following the Holy Rule of S. Benedict the soul tends as much as possible to a solitude, both interior and exterior, avoiding the tumult of action, so that thus, not only occasions of sins are avoided, but also the soul is better enabled, immediately, and without impediment, to wait upon God. This being so, there is ordained in his Rule a general custody of the soul about her doings. To this effect are applicable those words of his, in the first degree of humility, where he says, " his disciple should have always before his eyes the fear of God, and by all means avoid letting Him go out of his memory; but keeping himself (omni hora) at all times from sin and vice, that is to say, of the thoughts, tongue, eyes, hands, and of selfwill, he should esteem himself continually to be under the eyes of God, looking down from heaven upon his deeds, in every place, remembering that they are reported to God by the Angels at all times."

Also, in the twelfth degree, he requires " that the Monk should, in every place and at all times, esteem himself guilty and faulty for his sins, and think of his being presented before the terrible judgment-seat of God." These, and other like words, show that he esteemed the progress of his disciple to be very much in this continual custody of the heart. Those who practise this well retain a tenderness of conscience amidst all those extroversions which, of necessity, come upon them.

The guard they then keep over themselves prevents any notable fault from escaping their observation. Such may ever say, out of the set times of prayer and recollection, that word of the spouse of the Canticles: "I sleep, but my heart watches." I sleep, that is, I cease for the time all elevation of the spirit towards God, but yet my heart is watchful of Him, and cares to keep itself in good disposition for Him, against fitting time for actual union.

2. Besides the continued watchfulness over thoughts, words and actions in contemplative persons, it must be said also that their deeply grounded affection to God, which draws them ever inward, causes them to be less capable of notable faults. What seem to be faults may often be none at all, as lacking any evil principle in the will, and being wholly devoid of any malice. Faults generally proceed from inordinate attachment to the having our own will and desire. But, through the profoundness of their recollections, dulling and morti-

fying all other affections than those relating to God, contemplative persons do not incur these defects. Sometimes what seems defective to men is meritorious before God, being done purely for His honour, and the true advancement of the soul towards Him.

3. Again, the recollections, practised daily at set times by contemplative Religious, are of far more efficacy for searching into the soul, than the meditations of active livers. Although in them they do not go about to make an express examen of conscience, yet the effect of such an examen is there found; for the Divine Spirit within each one's conscience brings into the memory those perceptible sins and imperfections of any moment, that have been incurred since the last recollection. We all daily commit divers sins and imperfections, which we do not and cannot observe, be we never so spiritual, so secret and subtle they are. Of these the prophet says, "From my secret sins cleanse me, O Lord." Seven times a day falls the just man, yea, seventy times seven.

The contemplative soul purges herself of these defects, by elevating herself into God, as well as, or even better than, if she could, or had called them all to mind. For they commonly are of that kind that they cannot be amended, but by taking away and pulling up the habit of them by the root. This can be done in no way but the rising up of the soul out of nature and sensuality, into an estate more of the spirit, which in tract of time, indeed, she attains to by frequent and efficacious elevations of the spirit, in the times of recollection. This kind of redress those that have not an internal spirit cannot have. All that they can do is to cut off the branches, which daily spring forth again. They cannot take up the root by their exercises. The recollections of the contemplative discover to the soul the impediments between her and her God. These impediments are not so much the actual sins or imperfections which we commit, as the deliberate affections we have for them or their causes. These affections exist as perverse habitudes, deeply grounded in the soul; but they come to be corrected, or taken away, by the means above mentioned. Whereas the correcting only of the sins actually committed, and penitence for them, may leave the affection and habit much as they were before; and so long as this state of things exists, the soul can never make true spiritual progress.

During her recollection the soul finds herself corrected for divers irresignations: over-tenaciousness of will to one thing or other; and disorderly affections which are there presented to her mind; discovered to her by a certain presence, which she there finds, of God. He, being all light, enlightens the soul to see these inordinations, which of themselves are but darkness and nothing. The soul, of herself, is always in darkness as to those things. But when she comes to be enlightened about them by the divine presence and light, she profoundly produces and exercises resignation and conformity of her will to the Divine Will, thereby ever weakening and lessening the habits of irresignation and inordinate affections that are in her. But without such recollections the soul sits in darkness, and cannot see the impediments between her and her God, that ought to be corrected in her. Such impediments are discovered and corrected better by the immediate exercise of the will towards God, than by exercises in the imagination and discourse. Those who use these latter exercises regard the images of the matters whereof they discourse, more than they do God. They are less able to discern the said impediments than those who, in a manner, regard only God.

It is the regard and presence of God, and not of creatures or their images, that enlightens the soul for the discovering of hidden inordinate affections. Grosser and more palpable sins, actually committed, the soul can, by natural reason, discern and see, and such light and sight at least are common to contemplatives with the actives. On beholding them she purposes to amend in such and such particulars, for the time to come; the root or affection however remaining still unseen and unknown, ready again, when the soul is least aware, to break forth afresh into act.

This affection or root natural reason either cannot well discern, or cannot take away, as not having the proper means for doing so. The contemplative soul in her recollections makes no examen of her sins, or irresignations or inordinations, so far as God then pleases to have them discovered to her. The proceeding of the soul in this matter is thus described by a certain author: "As," says he, "one looking towards and upon a wall, that lies before his sight, thereby not only sees the wall, but also the things that are between him and the wall; even so, the soul regarding God, sees the impediments that are between Him and her." For such as lie lurking in her nature, and many such there be, God does not always discover them to the soul, yet even in such ignorance the souls gets out of them by degrees and in time.

She does this by transcension of all natural desires and inclinations, through the medium of recollection; quite as well too, as if they had been visibly discovered to her sight, and so she comes to be amended in them before she discerns or knows them. Nor is there any reformation in the soul, or perfection, but by the said means of getting out of the habitation of nature, and the inordinate desires of it, whether we discover them or discover them not. Many are discovered, and many not, which yet may be amended; for, in order to their being amended, it is not necessary they should be discovered.

Now there are such subtle, spiritual, and secret inordinations in our nature, that the rational powers are not able to find them out. Yet these rational powers are the senses by which alone the soul can discern, unless God enable her to know things by an extraordinary supernatural light.

This light He is not generally used to impart, but He rather concurs to or causes the reformation of the soul by the above mentioned means of transcension and the getting out of nature.

4. Another thing that helps to an examen of conscience for one in a contemplative course is this, that a sin or imperfection that would seem to be of little consequence to another, will seem great unto her, and will stick by her and gall her conscience, so that she need not seek to bear it in mind, nor to call it to mind. As for very minute and secret sins or imperfections, these are more profitably rubbed out (as spiritual writers teach) by acts of love and general contrition, or a regard and reflection upon God, rather than upon the sins themselves.

This, experience teaches us, is the best way of amendment for such minute and secret defects, which will never be amended by any other means. Much searching into them will only deject, obscure, and confound the soul, without any kind of profit or progress.

A contemplative soul, prosecuting such an enquiry, will either find her labour to be in vain, she being unable to find out anything but what she knew without it; or by doing so she will raise up scruples and causeless fears, finding or imagining sins and defects where none exist.

Light, however, is imparted in much fuller measure through the means of recollection, but the discovering by it of sins and defects is made rather to the spirit than to the rational powers. This light, also, is given rather in the entry or lower part of the state of contemplation, than in the purity or perfection of it; for that admits of no thoughts but of God Himself.

It is not, however, good for those, who have thus had made known to them their defects, to promise to God or themselves any hasty or certain amendment. They must be content, even for those lesser or more secret defects which they find in themselves, to expect length of time for a thorough reformation of them through grace. They will find it impossible to amend them otherwise, or sooner, by any industry or violence of their own.*

This Gertrude found by experience in herself, and said, "that she must amend as she could, and not as she would, and that she saw it was God's will that she should expect further time for a total amendment, and in the mean time that she should exercise patience with herself, mending by little and little, as she could," adding that, "if she had proceeded otherwise, she could not have amended herself in anything." The defects of contemplatives are commonly certain inordinate motions or inclinations of nature, which are to be reformed more by the divine grace and working than by man's promises, resolutions, or hasty violence.

Nothing of what has been said above is to be understood of the examination which is profitably made at longer intervals for the

* A l'egard de la vaine complaisance, je vous conseille de vous en défendre, mais sans inquietude—Il en faut souffrir : on n'arrache pas comme on veut cette mechante racine.

L'homme est composé de chair et d'esprit. Si l'esprit est fort, la chair est faible, et par malheur la partie faible, entraîne souvent la plus forte.—Surin. A Letter at the close of *Fondements Spirituelles*.

purpose of sacramental confession; for there the soul will more easily call to mind some thing or things done in all the space since her last confession. Some souls have enough, however, at times, and more than enough, to find out worthy and fitting matter for confession or absolution.

CHAPTER X.

THE ARIDITY IN PRAYER FELT BY GERTRUDE— HER TEMPTATION TO REITERATE FORMER CONFESSIONS.

It has been already stated in a former Chapter, that All-Hallowtide, in the year of her profession, was the date of Gertrude More's conversion, or entry into a true spiritual course. After Father Baker had given her his instructions, he left the matter with her, not at all knowing the serious way in which she took them, or that it might be a good while before she would get fully into the way he pointed out to her; nor did he know what she was doing until about the beginning of the following Lent, when she came to him, either purposely or by chance, and as he talked with her, he perceived that she was already entered on a good course, or at least well disposed for it. After that they met and conferred together more frequently, and she grew more and more settled in her course, being comforted and animated by him. His whole office, indeed, with her, was to animate her, and bear her up in it against all temptations that rose either from her own nature, or might proceed 'ab externo,' such as the sayings and practices of others to the contrary. He gave her also further general instructions, from time to time, and sometimes she had some particular question to ask, but was easily satisfied; for being now well settled in mind and in her spiritual course, she walked in it with courage, quietness, and satisfaction, followed her prayer at fitting seasons, and in fitting manner, spending the rest of her time in performance of her other obligations, and in discharge of her office of celleraria, into which office she was put on the change of the Abbess.

Although she was now in a good way, she was not without her sufferings, which were principally of an interior nature. Her prayer was that of affectionate aspirations. The sensible sweetness of these depends on the present disposition of the body, which is subject to alteration by reason of weather, and other natural causes. Those who can help themselves by meditation or immediate acts, are happy to be able to do so. Those who cannot are subject to what is called dryness or aridity. This aridity consists in a dulness or coldness of the sensitive will; but the soul abiding at her prayer, and doing the best she can, is enlightened in her spiritual intelligence, which is as capable of such illumination in the time of aridity, as in the time of sensible affection; and not only does the spiritual understanding of the soul receive light, but the will also receives strength and grace from God, no less, if not more, in time of aridity, than in the time it abounds in sensible affections.

Now, the essential profit of a soul consists in that light of love which is wholly spiritual, above the senses and rational powers. And by this means Gertrude therefore sped no less well in time of such sensible dryness, which was frequent with her, than she did in time of a better disposition for affective prayer. Before her conversion, not knowing that prayer made in the state aridity was of any use, because devoid of sensible affection, when such a case came upon her, she at once desisted from her prayer. Now she did not, but it was a good while before she had found the means of helping herself in the prayer of affection, and Father Baker would not prescribe to her any particular kind of prayer, but told her she must find it out by her own experience. The only things in matter of prayer he insisted on were these; first, that some mental prayer was necessary for her, though it must be her office to find what prayer would suit her; and second, that she was capable of mental prayer of some kind or other. This latter proposition was grounded on the authority of a well experienced father of the order of the Society of Jesus, Alvarez, in his third book, "De Spirituali Perfectione," where he affirms that there is no soul but what is capable of mental prayer, in some way or other. Besides this dryness within, her bodily health was but poor without; indeed, in her latter days so feeble, that, he was driven to be dispensed from fasting and from some abstinences. She was excused from rising at night for Matins, and from some of the day hours on occasions.

But the greatest cross she had to bear, was the burthen of a temptation to repeat the confessions of her former life, contrary to the resolute advice of her spiritual Fathers and Superiors. This temptation, and the greatness of it, she mentions in her writings. Much ado she had. She had already made some general confessions, but her searching head served her to find out points in her former life, which neither herself, nor perhaps any other, could solve. Even had they been able to do so, yet would not that have made an end of the matter, but she would still have found new conceits to the vexation of herself and others, so that there was no true remedy but for her utterly to desist from the confessing of all former matters, and standing to the good advice given her by her spiritual Fathers. But great difficulty had she so to do, because it seemed quite contrary to the light of her natural reason. The temptation was the most grievous to her before her conversion, she not being as yet come to the light and grace of prayer, nor consequently to any good obedience to God, or confidence in Him. She remained therefore little better than perplexed, and that with a grievous perplexity; for, on the one side, her spiritual Superiors had, out of good judgment, obliged her, in writing, (as far as they could by their authority,) not to reiterate, or reckon up, former confessions, but to rest satisfied with what she

had already made, and she durst not do the
contrary; on the other side, her natural reason seemed to demonstrate to her a necessity
of reiterations, though contrary to the decisions of Superiors. Thus she remained in
agony; for, as yet dealing with creatures, and
regarding her Superiors no otherwise, she was
not come to a subjection to them, either of the
understanding or of the will. Nor did she
ever come to it till she enjoyed a more immediate conversation with God. This grace
wrought in her a perfect subjection to Him,
and to all others for His sake. But before
this she was so miserable, that she often was
tempted with thoughts of regret that she had
ever entered Religion. " Nothing," says she,
in her writings, " has my Lord God left undone, which might win me wholly to Himself,
and make me despise myself, and all created
things, for His love. For, when I sinned, He
recalled me; He forsook me not when in my
misery, offending so shamefully His infinite
goodness; and that even after my entrance in
Religion, the happiness and worth of which I
did not yet know. Through this my ignorance I grew weary of bearing His sweet
yoke and light burden, which is heavy only

through our own fault, and not in itself. But it seemed so grievous and intolerable to me, that I wished often it might have been shaken off by me, pretending that it was so incompatible with my good, that I could hardly work out my salvation in this my state and profession. O, my God, Thou art witness that this is true. And so it continued with me for two years after I had in show forsaken the world, and the world indeed forsaken me.

"But did my Lord in these bitter afflictions forsake me? No, no! but He provided such a help for me, by means of a faithful servant of His, that quickly was my sorrow turned into joy, yea, into such an unspeakable joy, that it hath sweetened all the sorrows that have since befallen me; for, as soon as my soul was set into a way of tending to God, by prayer and abnegation, I found all miseries presently to disperse and come to nothing. Yea, even in the short space of five weeks my soul became so enamoured of the yoke of this my dear Lord, that, if it had been that I must have made not four only, but four thousand vows, to have become wholly dedicated to Him in the state of Religion, I should have embraced this state with more joy and content than ever I found in obtaining any other desired thing. This Thou knowest, O my God. For to my soul was discovered a kind of prayer I never before knew, a true means whereby I might love Thee, without end or measure."

Some time after her Profession, being much dissatisfied in soul, she sought to give it some satisfaction by making another general confession, though indeed she had done enough in that behalf at least at her Profession. And she being in that purpose, one morning knelt at the church grate, desiring to speak to Father Baker, who was then going to the altar. When he was come to her, she told him that she was about to make a general confession, and begged him to pray for her for that end, in his Mass. He said he would, but he could not choose but pity and smile at her proceedings, well knowing that that was not the way of getting satisfaction to her soul.

When she had made this confession, she was no better satisfied than before. Now, it is frequently the case, that good souls of both sexes, especially in the state of Religion, fancy they will find security and satisfaction of soul in making, or reiterating, confessions.

Yet these confessions, made without real necessity, do not only not satisfy or secure their souls, but rather obscure the light that is within them, and more estrange them from true confidence in God. The temptation to repeat her confessions still continued in Gertrude, even after she had become more settled and satisfied in mind at her conversion.

But now, being entered on the way of divine love, the temptation, and all other accidents in their kind, co-operated to her good and to her promotion in spirit. She courageously resisted the temptation, and thereby increased in grace and strength. This proceeding of hers wrought in her a great resignation to God, engendering in her soul an increase of confidence and love towards Him. It abated in her the contrary spirit, that is to say, dejection, pusillanimity, scrupulosity, and servile fear, which formerly obscured her soul, and estranged her from familiarity with God, and from all true love and confidence in Him.

It was this defect which made her life, as to her interior, where the true life or happiness is alone to be found, most uncomfortable and wearisome, yea, more miserable than can be expressed. But now, having strength to resist her temptation, she became both inwardly and outwardly light-hearted, mistress of herself, as well as more pleasing to others by her free and merry exterior carriage. Only once, through some fright, caused by the sermons, sayings, or writings of another priest, she yielded more than she was wont to her temptation, and got Father Baker to yield to her, so far as to let her make a confession of one or two things of her former life, a thing she had no need to have done. She afterwards acknowledged her error in so doing, and the damage incurred thereby; for, by so doing she became somewhat weaker in her power of further resistance of the temptation, and more inclined to yield again to it.

She renewed her courage, however, and made good use of this error, being more resolute to resist for the time to come, although the temptation stuck to her, even at her last sickness and death. It was indeed, as it were, inherent in her nature, as it descended to her from her mother, who was a very good devout gentlewoman, but over-much subject to the humour of scrupulosity and sadness.

Such temptations as arise from the quality

of the bodily temperament commonly abide in some measure while the life lasts, but time and spiritual exercises much abate their vigour. That desolation and obscurity of soul which is the effect of a dulness or coldness in the exercise of the affections towards God, and is commonly termed a state of aridity, was bound up, so to speak, also with her bodily temperament; and though modified by spiritual exercises, was a trial to her, more or less, so long as she lived.

This temptation, however, never prevailed on her so far as to make her desist, or slacken, in her tenderness to God by prayer, nor so as to make her remiss in the care of her external deportment.

Even amidst her obscurities, God did, as it were, secretly impart to her as much internal light as was necessary, though not with such clarity and satisfaction as nature desired, and which at other times she enjoyed. The want of the comfort of her usual light was to her a matter of great resignation; for this light clears the understanding, enabling it plainly to discern God and divine things. Whereas the purely spiritual light, when it does not descend at all into the rational powers, is a light hardly perceptible to the soul.

As these sufferings were of an inward nature, they caused a greater transformation, being patiently accepted, than any external sufferings could do, for these latter do not pierce so deeply into the soul as do matters that are of their own nature internal. The two special temptations which have been mentioned were of great profit to Gertrude, as a discipline to purify her soul, though they proceeded more from her own natural temperament than from any extraordinary dispensation of God.

He does not usually lay any great crosses or mortifications on His young and tender scholars, but thinks it sufficient for them to bear such as either their temperament of body, or their former evil and unmortified habits, together with their natural blindness, produce for them. Besides these sufferings, which came to her from the nature of her temperament, God was pleased, during the last two years, to try her with a much more searching discipline.

It sometimes happens that, in His own secret counsel, Almighty God permits good men to persecute other good men. To those who are persecuted He gives patience and resignation upon such persecution, and both persecutors and persecuted are guided and impelled in it by a true zeal for what is good, so that all is arranged for the merit and good of both. Hence we read of divers Saints that persecuted one another, yet such doings were not derogatory to the sanctity of either side.

The difference and variance between them proceeded from ignorance of some circumstances on one side or the other. These not appearing, and God not revealing them, each side proceeded conscientiously according to what they knew by natural reason. Consequently merit might be on both sides, and no rancour or breach of charity between them, notwithstanding the contention and variance, each side esteeming itself, and that with good probability, to be in the right. Nevertheless, it is no doubt much more painful to a good soul to be persecuted, or held in doubt by good men, than it is to be so by the evil. In a certain sense it is an honour to be persecuted by the evil, and the plain injustice of the persecution makes some amends for its bitterness. But to be held in doubt, or persecuted by the good, has no solace in it, unless directly from God, especially for a fearful heart.*

It came to pass, then, that certain Benedictine fathers, having authority and charge of this Nunnery in which Gertrude lived, and being very zealous to perform their spiritual duties well, began to call in question the method of her prayer, and the goodness of its nature.

This became an occasion of notable affliction and probation to Gertrude, and to some others her companions who followed the like spiritual course. It is very difficult for

---

* Father Surin, S.J., in his sixteenth Letter on Feasts, says thus of himself:

"La plus grande partie de ma conduite n'est pas au gré de ceux, de qui je depends, et ce qui est le fruit et l'emploi le plus doux de mon esprit passe dans le leur pour des reveries et pour une perte de temps. J' experimente ce que je vous ai dit souvent, que ce qui est pour les uns une grande sagesse, et ce qui est le plus precieux de leur bien, est tenu par d'autres pour folie. Dieu veut que nous demeurions soumis, et qu'encore que nos cœurs ne se puissent joindre à leurs idees, ils soient néanmoins dépendants de leur autorité, selon l'ordre legitime, qu'il a établi dans son royaume, dont nous sommes trop heureux d'être les sujets."

those who, in their own persons, have only had experience of the lower exercises of prayer, to esteem at proper value a prayer that is purely spiritual. Indeed, accustomed as they are only to the palpable exercise of discourse with images, the higher kind of prayer escapes their apprehension, which is yet gross, and seems to them no prayer at all, but an idle delusion. Several instances are given us in history of the suspicions with which men, only used to meditation, have regarded spiritual prayer.

There lived once in Spain a Religious man of the Society of Jesus, whose name was Baltazar Alvarez, whom it pleased God, after some years spent by him in meditation, to call to a sublime kind of spiritual prayer. This prayer was void of discourse, being grounded on motions of the will made by the Divine Spirit, which abundantly supplied for the lack of discourse.

In this kind of prayer, he for some years wholly exercised himself with much profit internal and external.

He also intimated the nature of his prayer to divers others of his order whom he thought to be capable of such prayer, commending it to them as the most profitable.

He had good opportunity to do this because he was a man of some authority in his Order, being a rector of a college. He was also well esteemed both for sufficiency of learning and talents, and for his virtues and devoutness of spirit. Through his intimations, strengthened by the virtues of his exemplary life, he drew many of his Order to the same kind of spiritual prayer. These not only themselves practised this prayer, but also, upon occasions, extolled this manner of prayer before others. Some, not rightly apprehending the nature of the prayer, spoke somewhat erroneously concerning it, either not being really apt for such prayer, or unable to express themselves in proper terms concerning the nature of it. Some, perhaps, going too far in their extolling of this prayer, debased the exercise of Meditation. These exercises caused others of the Order not only to call in question, but also to condemn, such a kind of prayer, especially for the practice of persons of their Order. They affirmed also that Father Baltazar meant to introduce his form of prayer into the Order, to the exclusion of Meditation, and the causing of much trouble and confusion in the Order, if not the subversion of it. The complaints of these zealous persons, about this form of prayer, were brought before the general of the order, who took measures for examining Father Baltazar's prayer.

Accordingly, some persons of worth were appointed for this task, and he was examined. He answered the examiners both by words and writing very religiously and satisfactorily in the matter. The conclusion come to was that this prayer was approved of by authority, not only for his own practice, but also for that of others that had a call to it.

For God does not call all to such a prayer, nor those that are called, in the beginning of their Religious course, but usually after some good time spent in the exercise of Meditation and vocal prayer.

This Father Baltazar lived in the time of S. Teresa; she in her writings confessed to have received great light and benefit in spiritual matters. This prayer being approved of he persevered in it till his blessed death, and has ever since been held by the Order to have been a very holy man, much honour and regard being paid to the monument where his body lies interred.

Father Baltazar's manner of prayer was approved only for those who had a call from God to it, not for general practice in the Order, which has by its institute another kind of prayer, that of Meditation.

CHAPTER XI.

HER SICKNESS AND LAST END.

The pain that Dame Gertrude felt in having suspicion thrown upon her, because of the manner of her prayer, was the greatest she had ever had to endure. She being naturally fearful, it took more hold of her than it would have done with another. And yet she knew from the ill success she had had in Meditation, which neither gave any remedy for her internal wants, nor enabled her to overcome herself without, that such a method of prayer was not suitable for her. Considering these things, and the good success both within and without of her present prayer, her fears somewhat abated, and she prepared in writing an account of her prayer for examination. The agitation that was made against her internal course, and that of certain other members of the house who had been under the guidance of Father Baker, was kept up for nearly two years. Then a certain venerable Father, who had been Confessor to Dame Gertrude when in England, came over to discourse with her and with Very Rev. Father Baker upon the matters which were then in debate concerning her spiritual course. He, being a man of excellent parts, and of sufficient talents to discuss things clearly and substantially, was deputed by the general Chapter which was to be held upon Monday, 1st of August, 1633, to make a clear inspection of all difficulties, and give a faithful account of all to the Reverend Fathers assembled in Chapter. The two Fathers, together with Dame Gertrude, and some others of the Nuns, consulted and conferred together, and gave so good an account of their proceedings, that the spiritual course they had held was confirmed and established by acts of the general Chapter.

Public thanks were given to Very Rev. Father Baker for the care he had taken of those pious souls under his conduct, and for his indefatigable pains in leaving them such rules and instructions as might serve to perpetuity for a happy direction in the Convent.

During the time of this conference Gertrude was indisposed, but still able to do all that was necessary for the composing of matters.

The very next day she fell sick, having taken from others the infection of the small pox. Her sickness increasing, within two days after she was seized she was carried from her cell to the Infirmary, where she remained until her death. During the course of her sickness, her total application was to keep her soul and heart fixed upon the divine object of her love, after which she vehemently aspired. As to exterior things, she little regarded them, knowing how ill they deserve any value or esteem, imitating the example of S. Romuald, founder of the Order of the Camaldulenses, who follow the Rule of S. Benedict. This holy man led a Religious and wholly eremitical life for a hundred years, being one hundred and twenty years old when he died.

Perceiving that his end drew near, he shut himself up in a more private cell, which he caused to be made for the purpose, and there ended his days in solitude and silence, denying all access to his disciples, and attending only to God and his interior in his last moments, without receiving any assistance from man at his death. Truly such silent deaths have been those of most perfect Saints, though some have been necessitated by the humble request of their disciples, or by a divine impulse and illumination, to speak something for the edification and encouragement of their subjects. They died practising silence without and within, in union with God, so long as they had their senses. Commonly they have enjoyed them to the last breath. Such was the death of the most holy Father S. Benedict, who, though the founder of so great an Order, and having his disciples about him, even until the departure of his soul from his body, yet we read not of any speech made by him to them. When he knew he was about to depart, being very feeble through sickness and age, he caused himself to be carried to the Church, where he had appointed a grave to be made for himself. Then, rapt in prayer to God, he rendered up his most blessed spirit, his disciples being present. If such were the way of meeting death, used by holy and perfect souls, and even of some superiors and founders of great Orders, who had spent many years in a Religious life, what ought younger disciples of the spiritual life to do, but wholly to attend to their interior, so far as obedience and necessity shall permit? Gertrude More seems to have quite looked forward to the possibility of an early death, and prepared herself for it.

These words occur towards the close of a book she wrote. "I will sing unto Thee of mercy and judgment all the days of my life, wishing always that Thy Will, which is justice itself, may be wholly and perfectly accomplished in me Thy sinful creature. Let me live as long as it pleaseth Thee, or die in the beginning of these my desires of love; send sickness or health, sudden or lingering death, poverty or abundance, good fame, or that I be by the world despised: and, in fine, in all things do with me as is according to Thy Will and most for Thy honour." These and other words to the same effect, were uttered by her to God, plainly discovering a will resigned for death, which is the greatest matter for resignation in this life. She then, being in this disposition, was actually and suddenly surprised with the bodily sickness which proved to be her last, by which the occasion offered itself to her to practise what she had only before in will and resolution; as if God indeed meant to take her at her word, or had said to her according to the Gospel: "Ex ore tuo judico te." Thus, commonly the Divine Wisdom proceeds with a soul He loves, first disposing her interiorly for the probation, and afterwards sending her actually and externally what He had before prepared.

In Gertrude's book of confessions is a sweet picture of the happy internal state and purity of her soul. Her conscience is there laid open in the sight of God, she speaking with Him, by way of humble prayer and colloquy. Her " Cantum Cygnæum" or " Swan's Last Song," as it may be termed, because made by her not long before her last sickness, breathes with the same sweet tones, and shows an amorous love for death.

I.

Now but one wish have I, O Lord,
    That Thou of me dispose
E'en as Thou wilt in everything,
    Till death mine eyelids close ;—
Death, which my heart so much desires,
    For it will me procure
Those endless joys with Thee, my God,
    Where I shall be secure.

II.

None from me, then, can take my Lord,
    But everlastingly
I shall enjoy my only Good,
    And His shall ever be.
Drawn close to Him by bands of love,
    Which nought can e'er untie;
They shall remain as permanent
    As is eternity.

III.

O happy hour, when wilt thou come,
    And set my spirit free?
That I may fly to Him above;
    Far from earth's misery.
There, gazing in His glorious face,
    With all that Him adore,
I then shall sing His sweetest praise,
    In joy for evermore. Amen.

As her sickness continued and increased, and she came nearer to death, so accordingly did the matters of resignation increase. She, on her part, was faithful in resigning herself to the pains and dolours of her sickness, to death, to purgatory, and, in general, to the Divine Will and judgments, both for time and eternity.

As she was careful to observe the divine inspirations, and attend within her soul to God, so now, when death approached, her zeal increased, and in a still closer manner she conversed with God. When in health she was wont to say to Father Baker, touching death, that we ought to live as we would die, and then to die as we have lived. But for her more particular behaviour during her last sickness, it is recorded by the Very Reverend Father Cuthbert Horsley, who ministered to her the Sacrament of Extreme Unction. He says thus of her in a letter to Father Baker. "If patience, resignation, and confidence in God can give testimony of a good conscience to die well, she died as happily as ever I saw any creature in my whole life. When I was called in to give the last sacraments, I spoke with her alone, and asked her these questions, viz. :—' Are you content to suffer these afflictions laid upon you by Almighty God for the satisfaction of your sins?' She answered, ' With all my heart.' ' Are you content to die, if it please God to take you in this sickness?' 'With all my heart.' 'Do you forgive all your Religious Sisters, and all the world, for whatsoever they have offended you in? Do you also desire forgiveness of them all?' 'Yes, with all my heart.' 'Do you desire the Sacrament of Extreme Unction?' 'Yes, I truly do.' Then I called in the Nuns and gave her this Holy Sacrament, and afterwards the Plenary Absolution, (which we have by participation from Spain,) and performed some other ceremonies according to the rubrics of the Ritual. This done, I gave her my blessing, which she received with great signs of joy, and then I went out. After this I saw her no more, but still enquired how she did, and answer was given that she remained in the same peace and quiet, until her very last breath.

"I have given you as particular a relation of her disposition to die well as I can; my Lady Abbess can give you a more clear account, for she was almost continually with her, both before and after. She certainly gave as great signs of resignation and confidence in God as could be seen in any one, which, without all doubt, is an evident token of her being in favour and grace of His Divine Majesty, whose fruition I doubt not she enjoys, which of His infinite mercy may He grant us also." These are the words of Father Cuthbert, in his letter of October 20, 1633.

Dame Anne More was one of the four that was appointed to tend her, towards the end of her sickness, for the rest of the Nuns, on account of the infection of the disease, were forbidden to resort to her. This Nun, writing to a kinswoman of theirs, expresses herself thus:—" It was my good fortune to be with Dame Gertrude during the time of her sickness, and when her happy soul departed. I beseech Jesus to grant me grace to imitate her innocent life, that I may have so happy a death. Truly she has left so great edification to us who remain behind her, that my poor soul is not able to express it. The pains I took about her, in her sickness, are not to be compared to the great comfort I received, in seeing such patience in so loathsome a sickness as hers was.

"Verily I have seen in her a Job on a dunghill, a Lazarus with his sores, an Angel in Paradise, so resigned to the Will of God, so willing to die, so ready to suffer more if It pleased God, having so firm a confidence, with humility, in the Divine mercy, always praying and calling on the sweet name of Jesus."

Sister Hilda Percy was one who waited on her last illness. Her words are these:— "Her sickness began to appear the 29th of July; though she had been a fortnight before much indisposed as to meat and sleep, yet she was able to go up and down the house till the 1st of August. On this day she found herself so weak, that she was not able to rise to hear Mass, and that same day she went to the Infirmary. The doctor, coming to her, could not find what her sickness was, nor perceive any fever, until the small-pox appeared, but we saw she suffered much anguish, and this with admirable patience, from the first hour until the last breath. Thus she continued, the small-pox coming out for ten or eleven days successively, and the danger still increasing. I, being in the same room with her, and being about her, heard her asked whether she desired to speak with Father Baker, or would have anything signified to or sent to him concerning her? She answered, '*None*, but to give him thanks a thousand times for that he had brought her to such a state, that she could confidently go out of this life without speaking to any man.'

"Confession day being come, (which was then on every Saturday,) she desired a priest to come to her, and at that time there was none to be had here but a stranger, whom we had never known before. He being come in she humbly went to confession, but could not communicate by reason of an extraordinary stiff phlegm, which afflicted her, upon her first coming to the Infirmary, and continued until the breath went out of her body. The doctor, coming frequently to her, gave her many things, which she took with great patience, except one syrup, that seemed very loathsome to her, which she desired for God's sake to be given her no more.

"To this I immediately answered her, for God's sake she must take it, her recovery being of great concern to us, whereupon without reply she took it, submitting as often as it was given her, which was every half hour. She never complained of her pains, but as we plainly discerned, they were great; she in all sincerity told us where she suffered, when less and when more. Sometimes she called, and said, 'I burn, I burn within, but all else is nothing in comparison of what I suffer in my throat.' In all her sickness she was never troubled at anything that was done or said about her, except once. It being observed by one that she suffered much pain with great patience and resignation, she happened to say to her: 'God be praised, Dame, that you leave us so good an example to bear what suffering is laid upon us.' At which, with a disturbed countenance, she shook her head, and said: 'Hold your peace.' But the person replied in her hearing, for at that time she was doing something about her which caused her much pain: 'Though you are not willing to hear it, yet we ought to take example by it;' to which she made no reply. She often desired to lie quiet; wholly giving herself to God; praising His Divine Majesty, who never laid upon His servants more than they were able to bear. At other times she desired to be recreated, which she did heartily and freely to our comfort, signifying how those recreations did her much good, by which we perceived her peace both of mind and soul.

"Upon some occasion, which I do not well remember, a dear friend of hers said to her: 'Though your life be very grateful unto me, yet I dare not so much as beg it of Almighty God.' She hearing this, said joyfully : ' That it is the very best of all ;' for both desired that God's Holy Will might be done in all things.

"She, finding herself growing worse, desired to have the last sacraments administered to her; but we, not perceiving any present danger, put it off for some four or five days, during which time she never spoke more of it, but left it to God's Providence and our care, we having all things in readiness against the time.

"Upon the 16th of August, in the morning, my Lady Abbess sent word that we, (the four appointed to help her,) might, if we would, come to the Choir to communicate, and asked her whether she desired that they should receive the Body of our Lord for her Viaticum ? to which she replied, ' Yes, for God's sake,' and so they did. When we returned she grew worse, as she had divers changes before. She spent all that day very quietly and piously, stirring little until night. Then she desired to be held up a while, but was not able to continue long in that posture, but laid herself down, listening to some holy aspirations.

Sometimes I begged she would remember me in her prayers, and she answered me confidently that she would when she got to heaven. The like she did when she was several times spoken to for all the Community. To conclude, she spent her time very devoutly, with great edification to all that were present. Towards twelve o'clock at night she called for something which she took, and after that lay quietly, yet seeming to draw very near to death. As she began to grasp me frequently, I pronounced aspirations into her ears, to which she answered as long as she could speak. When she could not utter a word more, she kissed the Crucifix, and lifted up her hands, and so happily reposed in our Lord upon the 17th of August, 1633. Much more might be said of her sickness and patience, but for my part I am not able to speak of her what she deserves. With regard to the nature of her distemper, you have heard of it. I will, however, touch on one point, and that is, how most odious and loathsome it was, very near the plague. Indeed her flesh, both inwardly and outwardly, did rot away, so that she had much ado to keep the flies from making their nests in her face, and eating while alive. As she did not at all complain, I asked her whether she felt them, to which she answered, 'Yes.'" Thus far the relation of Sister Hilda.

The last witness of her sickness was the Lady Abbess, her Superior, Very Rev. Mother Catherine Gascoigne, a person with whom she had the greatest freedom. She gives this relation of her.

"During the time of her last sickness, which was not long, but wonderfully painful, she has left us a good example of patience, resignation, and confidence in God, as every one affirms that has had anything to do about her, or who were present with her in the time of her sickness.

"As she had been faithful to God in prosecuting the happy spiritual course, which Father Baker was the means of leading her to, so she stood constantly in the practice and principles of it all the time of her last sickness to the very last moments of her life. For that happy exercise of love and confidence, which, with so much diligence and fidelity, during her life she so purely followed, the Divine Goodness was pleased to give her grace to continue until her last expiration. I often went to her in the time of her sickness, to afford her what solace I could, for the ease of her pains, which were very grievous. But, instead of comforting and refreshing her, I was much comforted myself to see her so patient, so truly resigned to the Divine Will for all things without exception, so humbly confident in the goodness and mercy of God, in a word, so sweetly and happily disposed for heaven, that I know not how to express it. When she had been some five or six days ill, and her throat was growing so bad that she feared it would hinder her speech, she desired to have Father Horsley come to hear her confession. He did go, and gave her a Plenary Indulgence, but her disease was such that she neither could, nor was it thought fit that she should, communicate then, and much less afterwards. Ever after that confession she seemed to have her soul settled in such peace, that she had now no more to do but to resign herself to God Almighty's Will, neither fearing to die nor desiring to live, but only to submit to her Supreme Master, both living and dying. I asked her sometimes, when I was to write to Douay, whether she would have me to say anything concerning her to anyone there, where they were assembled for a General Chapter, and whether she desired not to speak with Father Baker, or her former Confessor, when in England, or with any other of our Fathers; for I told her how I was certain that any of them would come over to her, to which she answered, '*No;* but that she humbly desired, for God's sake, all their prayers.' She said, if anything in the world troubled her conscience, she could have spoken to Father Maurus as well as to any other. She seemed to have been very pleased with him, saying he had done his Office for her as well as any man in the world could do. Some three or four days before she died, when we feared she would not escape, I went to her one night, as I used to do, and thought to let her know she was in danger, and so told her. She seemed not to be the least moved or daunted, but by her words and actions shewed all possible signs of resignation.

"I told her how loath I was to part with her, and what a loss I should have. She, perceiving me troubled, answered, 'Oh, do not fear, doubt not but God will supply.' I said again, 'If it must be, His holy will be done, I dare not resist.' 'That is the best of all,' said she, 'His will be done.' Then, by accident, we fell into some discourse concerning Father Baker, upon which she said, 'God reward him for the good he has done to the house, and for all the good he has done to my poor soul. What a blessed thing that he should bring a soul to such a pass, that, coming to die, she hath nothing to trouble her, but can rely wholly upon God.' Then, speaking of the Divine Goodness, and His disposition of all things, and particularly of His mercy towards her: 'God,' said she, 'has given me peace in my soul, and what can one desire more, coming to die? His sweet will be done in me, and in all things. Methinks I have nothing to do, but to leave myself wholly to Him.' These were her words as near as I can remember, and more to the same effect did she say, plainly showing how truly resigned she was, both to her own particular lot, and to all things concerning the house, for she confidently relied upon Almighty God's providence in the care of both.

"Upon another occasion she said, 'There are a great many fine souls in this house, and I doubt not that God Almighty will have many a saint out of it.' She again, two or three times in her sickness, noticed to me how tender and careful every one was of her, and how charitable and loving all were to one another. Upon the Assumption of our Blessed Lady, the physician wished, with all speed, the Blessed Sacraments might be administered to her, and so Father Cuthbert came in as soon as Evening Song was ended, which for that cause was advanced. She received them with good devotion, and he also gave her then the last absolution, which is usually given at the point of death; for we all thought she was very near it, and the doctor had said she could not live past midnight. The infection so increased in contagiousness as she drew near death, that though I meant not to have left her as long as she lived, yet it was fitting I should forbear coming to her, through regard for the safety of the community. Besides, I was very sick that night, and the doctor said how I had ventured too far, so that from this time she had no more than the four appointed to tend her, and we expected every minute that she would expire, yet she lived all the next day and until midnight again, and the most part of that time, as I conceive, she spent in prayer, for the nearer to death she approached, the quieter she lay, and the less desirous she was of speaking, except only at times to recreate herself. The night before she died, there came to our convent her former confessor and another with him. Word was carried to the Infirmary that he and Father Baker were come, and one of the four asked if she desired to speak to Father Baker, but she answered, 'No.' Then they asked her if she would not speak to the former Confessor, and she, speaking a little more loud and earnestly, said, '*No, with no man.*'

"Then they asked her if she would have God, and she answered, 'Yes, with all my heart.' This showed how confidently she died, relying wholly upon God; continually, as far as could be gathered by her exterior behaviour, all the time of her sickness, raising herself towards Him in such sort as she could.

"There was no impediment betwixt Him and her, she always by love aspiring towards the Divine Majesty. She fell sick the very day our Fathers went from hence to Douay, but was indisposed some days before, when she and I parted at the grate with Father Baker, and she went sick to her chamber. The next day she was carried into the Infirmary, and on the 17th of August, after midnight, the Community being at Matins, about one of the clock, she rendered her happy soul to God, after whom she sighed and thirsted with so much desire and love, that she esteemed all her sufferings nothing for His sake."

Dame Gertrude More thus died aged twenty-seven years complete, her birth-day being the 25th of March. Her death took place in the tenth year of her receiving the Religious habit, and almost eight years she had followed the spiritual course taught her by Father Baker. She lies buried in the Monastery of Dremea, in Cambray.

The House in Brussels, which gave the Superior to that of our Lady of Comfort at Cambray, was founded by Lady Mary Percy. It has been now removed to East Bergholt, near Colchester.

The Abbey of Stanbrook represents that of Cambray. S. Benedict's Priory, Colwich, is the Paris House founded from Cambray in 1651, and S. Scholastica's, at Atherstone, is a daughter of S. Benedict's Priory, at Colwich.

PUBLISHED BY RICHARDSON AND SONS,
26, Paternoster Row, London; and Derby.

Spiritual Letters of Father Surin, S.J., First Series. Translated by Sister M. Christopher, Order of S. Francis. With a Preface by Father Francis Goldie, S.J. Edited by the Rev. H. Collins, price 4s. 6d.

These most beautiful Letters, addressed to Religious, and to devout people living in the world, are a golden treasury of maxims and instructions for the spiritual life.

The Cistercian Fathers, or Lives and Legends of certain Saints and Blessed of the Order of Citeaux, translated by the Rev. Henry Collins. With a Preface by the Rev. W. R. Brownlow, M.A., one of the Editors of "Roma Sotterranea." FIRST SERIES, price 4s.

The Cistercian Fathers. SECOND SERIES, price 4s. 6d.

Devotions of Dame Gertrude More, Rearranged by the Rev. H. Collins, cloth, red edges, 1s.

The Divine Cloud, with Notes and a Preface, by Father Augustin Baker, O.S.B., the whole edited by the Rev. Henry Collins, printed on toned paper, small 8vo, price 4s.

St. Bernard and his Work. A Discourse delivered during the Public Festivities at La Trappe of N. D. Du Desert, near Toulouse, on the Feast of St. Bernard, 1874, by the Rev. P. Causette, Vicar-General, and Superior of the Priests of the Sacred Heart, at Toulouse. Translated from the French by the Right Rev. Abbot Burder, O. Cist. (Permissu Superiorum.) Price 1s.

Praxis Synodi Diœcesanæ Celebrandæ. Ex Opere D. B. Gavanti Redacta. Editio Altera. Permissu Superiorum. 8vo, cloth lettered, red edges, price 3s.

Published by Richardson and Sons.

Mediæval Library of Mystical and Ascetical Works.

Select Revelations of S. Mechtild, Virgin, taken from the Five Books of her Spiritual Grace, and Translated from the Latin by a Secular Priest. Superfine Cloth, price 3s. 6d.

Meditations on the Life and Passion of our Lord Jesus Christ. By Dr. John Tauler, Dominican Friar. Translated from the Latin by a Secular Priest. Superfine Cloth, Price 6s.

The Book of the Visions and Instructions of B. Angela of Foligno, as taken down from her own lips by Brother Arnold of the Friars Minor. Now first translated into English by a Secular Priest of the Third Order of St. Dominic, Author of a translation of the Life of Ven. Grignon de Montfort. price 4s.

The Fiery Soliloquy with God, of the Rev. Master Gerlac Petersen, throwing light upon the Solid Ways of the whole Spiritual Life. Translated from the Latin by a Secular Priest, price 3s.

A Catechism for the Right Understanding of the Sacrifice and Liturgy of the Mass, for the Use of Schools. Compiled at the Request of Authority, by Mrs. Stuart Laidlaw. From a Work by the Rev. John Macdonald, Priest of the Catholic Church. Foolscap 8vo, price 2s. 6d.

Father Eudes, Apostolic Missionary, and his Foundations. 1601-1874. By. M. Ch. de Montzey. With a Brief of Approval addressed to the Author by His Holiness Pope Pius IX. Post 8vo, superfine cloth, price 4s. 6d.

Published by Richardson and Sons.

Heaven to All who Love. By the Abbe Nambride de Nigri. Translated from the French by Madame R. A. Vain, post 8vo., price 4s.

Meditations on the Way of the Cross. By L'Abbe H. Perreyve. Edited in English by a Priest of the Diocese of Birmingham. Superfine Cloth, price 2s.

Spiritual Works of Saint Francis Borgia. Cloth, price 1s.

Spiritual Consolation, or a Treatise on the Peace of the Soul, from the French of Pere Lomber, interspersed with various Instructions necessary for promoting the Practice of Solid Piety, by the Authoress of "The Ursuline Manual." Small 8vo, Superfine Cloth, price 4s.

The Dollingerites, Mr. Gladstone, and Apostates from the Faith. A Letter to the Catholics of his Diocese, by Bishop Ullathorne, demy 8vo, price 3d.

The Mistress of Novices Instructed in her Duties: or, a Method of Direction for the use of Persons charged with the Training of Souls in Christian and Religious Perfection. Translated from the Second Edition by the Rev. F. Ignatius Sisk, of Mount St. Bernard's Abbey, price 4s.

The Christian Trumpet; or, Previsions and Predictions about impending General Calamities, the Universal Triumph of the Church, the Coming of Antichrist, the Last Judgment, and the End of the World. Compiled from the Writings of the Saints and eminent Servants of God, and other approved ancient and modern sources, by a Missionary Priest. With Superior's Permission. Price 5s.

Published by Richardson and Sons.

Just Published, Demy 18mo, handsomely bound in cloth,

Price **6ᵈ** each.

Catholic Tales for the Young.

NEW SERIES.

Morning and Evening Star.	The Holy House.
Christmas Dinner.	A Tale of the Crusaders.
Hawthorn Bush.	Maurice's Trials.
Pearl Lost & Found.	Carry's Trials.

☞ *Will be followed by others uniform in type and binding.*

The Paradise of the Earth; or the True Means of finding Happiness in the Religious State, according to the Rules of the Masters of Spiritual Life. Originally published with the approbation of several French Bishops, and many Religious Superiors and Directors, by Abbe Sanson, Author of "the Happiness of Religious Houses. Now first translated by Rev. Father Ignatius Sisk, St. Bernard's Abbey. One vol., small 8vo., 500 pages, price 5s.

Our Lady of Lourdes.—The History of the Miraculous Sanctuary of Our Lady of Lourdes, in the Department of the Upper Pyrenees, France, translated by the Rev. Father Ignatius Sisk, O.C., of St. Bernard's Abbey, Leicestershire, from the French of Henry Lasserre, with his special permission. A work honoured through 25 Editions, with a Brief of Approval addressed to the Author by Pope Pius IX., price 5s.

www.ingramcontent.com/pod-product-compliance
Lightning Source LLC
Chambersburg PA
CBHW032148160426
43197CB00008B/822